The
Vegetarian
Mother
and
Baby
Book

The Vegetarian Mother and Baby Book

ROSE ELLIOT

PANTHEON BOOKS
NEW YORK

LIBRARY OF CONGRESS CATALOGING-IN-PUBLICATION DATA
Elliot, Rose.
The vegetarian mother and baby book.
Includes index.
1. Pregnancy—Nutritional aspects. 2. Infants—Nutrition.
3. Vegetarian cookery. I. Title. II. Title: The vegetarian mother and baby book.
RG559.E45 1986   613.2'62   86-853
ISBN 0-394-54695-4
ISBN 0-394-74620-1 (pbk.)

Manufactured in the United States of America
10 9 8 7 6

Contents

Part 2
The Recipes

Appendix

Acknowledgments

I'd like to express my love and gratitude to my mother, Joan Hodgson, whose mothering was the pattern and model for my own; and to my husband and three daughters, without whom this book certainly wouldn't have been written. My grateful thanks, too, to all the people who have encouraged and helped me in writing this book: to the Vegetarian Society (U.K.) for getting me started (and especially Dr. Alan Long), and to Fontana (and especially Helen Fraser) for publishing the U.K. edition of *Rose Elliot's Vegetarian Baby Book;* also to my agent, Vivienne Schuster for her enthusiasm and support; to Dr. Alan Long for advice on nutrition; and to Gill Thorn, my antenatal teacher when I had Claire, and dear friend ever since, for reading through the manuscript and making many valuable suggestions. My special thanks, too, to Wendy Wolf of Pantheon for making this U.S. edition possible, particularly for all her bright new ideas and suggestions, and to Juliet Annan, also of Pantheon, for putting my rather British-sounding manuscript through all the changes necessary to make it right (I hope!) for the United States.

PART

1

The
Vegetarian
Diet
for
Healthy
Mothers
and
Babies

Introduction

Producing healthy children is one of the most important—and certainly most demanding—occupations most of us will do in a lifetime. Considering this, many people—myself included—take on the responsibility in a very carefree way. Now, however, the emphasis is increasingly being placed on preparation for pregnancy and childbirth, with particular attention to diet: healthy parents produce a healthy baby.

The question of diet is an especially important one for vegetarian parents and parents-to-be. If you are vegetarian and pregnant, or planning to start a family in the near future, you may well wonder whether such a diet can supply all the nutrients necessary for producing a healthy baby. Indeed, you, or if not you, probably your mother or mother-in-law, may also wonder whether such a diet is actually nutritious enough to sustain you and your partner over a long period of time!

To set your mind at rest right away, the answer to all these questions is yes, and it may encourage you to know that vigorous, lively fifth-generation vegetarian and vegan babies are now being born. It is, however, helpful for any vegetarian to have access to a few crucial facts about nutrition, and particularly important for a pregnant or about-to-be-pregnant vegetarian or one who is caring for a baby or toddler. And that is the reason I have written this book, which I do hope you will find helpful.

How a Vegetarian Diet Can Supply All the Nutrients Needed for Health

First, perhaps it would be helpful to define what is usually meant by the words *vegetarian* and *vegan*. A vegetarian diet generally means one that excludes meat, fish, and poultry and products derived from these, such as meat stock and fats (for example, lard, drippings, suet) and gelatine, but includes eggs, milk, and dairy products. A vegan diet is stricter and excludes all animal products.

As I have already said, both these diets can supply all the nutrients necessary for health. Indeed, there are many people who would go further and say that not only can they do this, but they are also healthier than a traditional meat diet because they bypass the saturated fat and unwanted hormones, antibiotics, and other undesirable additives commonly found in meat. Nevertheless, whatever we vegetarians think about eating animals, if we're fair-minded, we have to admit that meat and fish are concentrated sources of some essential nutrients. Although adequate amounts of these can be found in most vegetarian foods, on the whole we do not have such concentrated sources. So while a meat eater can be adequately nourished without knowing much about nutrition, if you're vegetarian or vegan, it's helpful to know a few simple facts so that you can be sure to base your diet on the most nutritious foods. If you do this, chances are you'll end up far healthier and more full of energy than any meat eater!

Throughout the following chapters, the nutritional values of foods have been taken from *The Composition of Foods,* by R. A. McCance and E. M. Widdowson (London: HMSO, 1960); from *Nutrition Almanac,* edited by John D. Kirschmann, Director, Nutrition Search, Inc. (New York: McGraw-Hill Book Co., 1979); and from *Jane Brody's Nutrition Book,* by Jane Brody (New York: W. W. Norton & Co., 1981).

The Essential Nutrients:
What They Are and
Where to Find Them

PROTEIN

This is the first thing most people worry about when they start thinking about vegetarian nutrition, which is understandable, since a vegetarian diet excludes two major sources of protein, meat and fish. However, getting sufficient protein is not such a problem as people imagine. In fact if a vegetarian diet contains sufficient B vitamins and calcium, it will almost certainly contain adequate amounts of protein as well, because the foods that contain these nutrients are also good (if in some instances unconventional) sources of protein. It's rather a case of "If you look after the calcium and B vitamins, the protein will look after itself"! Cereals, for instance, which are vital sources of the B vitamins thiamine, riboflavin, and niacin, also contain a significant amount of protein, which adds up over the course of the day. The same applies to legumes. Milk, yogurt, and cheese, which are rich in both calcium and B vitamins, are, as we all know, high in protein. Strict vegetarians, of course, do not eat dairy products, but, again, if they make the replacements necessary to make their diet adequate in B vitamins and calcium (as explained on pages 15–22 and 33), their diet, too, will contain sufficient protein.

Table 1 gives some examples of the protein content of the staple foods in a vegetarian diet, and in table B in the Appendix you will see how the protein in a typical day's eating adds up to provide more than the 44 grams or so that is the recommended daily allowance for women.

TABLE 1
SOURCES OF PROTEIN IN THE
VEGETARIAN/VEGAN DIET
(RDA: Average man, 70 g; average woman, 44 g; pregnant
woman, 74 g; lactating woman, 64 g; child up to age 5,
20–45 g)

FOOD	WEIGHT	PROTEIN (IN GRAMS)
2 slices whole-grain bread	1½ ounces	2.4
¼ cup raw millet	2 ounces	5.6
1 cup rolled oats, raw	1½ ounces	2.5
½ cup rolled oats, cooked	4 ounces	2.5
½ cup brown rice, cooked	3 ounces	4.0
¾ cup whole wheat pasta, raw	2 ounces	10.0
¼ cup wheat germ, untoasted	9/10 ounce	6.6
½ cup cooked lentils or beans	3½ ounces	8.0
1 cup lentil sprouts, raw	3½ ounces	8.5
½ cup cooked soybeans	3¼ ounces	10.0
½ cup soy flour, full fat	1¼ ounces	13.0
1 cup soy milk	8 ounces	8.0
1 piece tofu	3½ ounces	8.0
1⅓ cups low-fat cottage cheese, not packed	10 ounces	41.0
1 cup low-fat yogurt	8 ounces	13.0
1 cup low-fat milk	9 ounces	8.5
¼ cup skim-milk powder	½ ounce	8.5
Hard cheese	1½ ounces	11.0
1 egg	2 ounces	6.5
¼ cup almonds	1⅓ ounces	7.3
¼ cup Brazil nuts, cashew nuts, walnuts	1⅓ ounces	3–4.0
¼ cup peanuts	1⅓ ounces	9.4
1 tablespoon peanut butter	½ ounce	3.9
¼ cup sunflower, sesame, or pumpkin seeds	1⅓ ounces	10.1
1 tablespoon tahini	½ ounce	2.5

When considering the question of protein, it's important to remember that in addition to these sources, extra amounts can come from unexpected foods. An average size (8 ounces) potato, for instance, supplies 5 grams of protein; a cup of cooked broccoli supplies around 8 grams; and a medium-size apple and orange together supply 1.5 grams. These may not be traditional protein foods, but when this protein is mixed, over the course of a meal, with other, richer sources, it is just as valuable to the body.

Speaking of mixing protein, many vegetarians or would-be vegetarians worry because they have heard that in order for the diet to be adequate, it's essential to balance and complement protein foods. They worry, further, that the protein derived from vegetable sources, such as legumes, cereals, potatoes, and green vegetables, is not of such high quality as that obtained from animals and animal products. In particular, they may wonder whether there's a subtle "something" missing from a nonmeat diet that will adversely affect them, or, more particularly, their unborn child or future generations.

All protein, whether it be animal, cereal, legume, or potato, is made out of building blocks called amino acids. There are twenty-two of these, and the mixtures and proportions vary in different foods. These amino acids are necessary for proper growth and for repair of tissues. The body can actually make fourteen of these amino acids by using components from other foods, but there are eight that it cannot make, and these are called essential amino acids. In order to be adequate, a diet must contain these in sufficient quantities.

Many animal proteins contain these essential amino acids in roughly the right proportion for the body to use. The eight essential amino acids are also all found in nonanimal foods, but generally not in proportions that are as convenient for the body. Legumes, for instance, are rich in the amino acids isoleucine and lysine. In order to be able to use these, the body needs to be able to mix them with the amino acids tryptophan and methionine. Legumes do contain some tryptophan and methionine but not enough to marry up with all the isoleucine and lysine, so some of these amino acids are wasted. The same is true of cereals, nuts, and seeds, except that here the amino acids are the other way around. This group is rich in tryptophan and methionine and weak in isoleucine and lysine. (It's worth remembering, incidentally, that no animal protein, with the exception of breast milk, has perfect proportions either; only about 70 to 75 percent of the protein in beef and cow's milk is fully usable, and similar percentages are found in some vegetables and cereals, such as potatoes, soybeans, and oats.)

In actual fact, most people eat protein from more than one source at any meal. This means that the different essential amino acids are being supplied by a number of foods, and a deficiency of an amino acid in one food is very likely to be balanced without difficulty by an abundance in another. The protein groups that complement each other in this way are: legumes, cereals, nuts and seeds, and dairy products. When a protein from one of these groups is mixed with one from any other group, more protein from each of the protein foods can be used by the body. The whole is greater than the sum of the parts. The interesting thing is that, far from being a highly taxing job, mixing proteins is the most natural thing in the world. In fact, in a normal diet you'd be quite hard-pressed *not* to mix your proteins in the course of a meal! Think of lentil soup and a roll, red kidney bean salad in pita bread, a cheese sandwich, pasta with Parmesan, breakfast muesli with milk and nuts. One of the most interesting examples of complementary proteins is hummus, a traditional age-old food that consists of an almost perfect combination of a legume (chick-peas) with a seed (tahini) that's normally eaten with a cereal (pita bread)! If you plan normal meals—the kind that most people want to eat— you'll automatically mix your proteins and needn't worry about this.

FIBER

Fiber is not a nutrient, but it is vital to health. It is the structural part of fruits, vegetables, and cereals; that is, it is the cellulose, woods, and gums that hold them together. Fiber serves as a kind of rationing device, beginning in the mouth, because it has to be chewed, and there's a limit to the amount of chewing anyone can do. So you might say fiber is nature's way of preventing us from becoming fat, and certainly people on "primitive" diets containing a high amount of fiber are beautifully slim. But the role of fiber doesn't end there. Just as we had to bite our way through the fiber to eat the food, so our digestive juices have to work their way through the fiber in order to extract all the goodness mixed up with it. Therefore, our bodies are able to cope with the nutrients gradually, as they're drawn out. The whole process is methodical and systematic. Then, as the fiber travels along the digestive tract, it absorbs liquid and becomes bulky, like a sponge. Thus the muscles of the intestine can get a good grip and move its contents along smoothly, quickly, and efficiently.

If the fiber is taken out of foods, these natural safeguards are lost. Sugar is perhaps the ultimate example of this. In its natural state sugar is found in fruits and vegetables and in particular in sugar cane and sugar beet, a tough root. If it wasn't for modern refining methods, it would be impossible to eat more than a sprinkling of sugar even if you chewed all day long. As it is, it's easy to eat a bar of chocolate or several cookies and hardly notice it.

So instead of the digestive system having to work its way slowly through the fiber to ease the goodness out, with refined foods this natural regulator has been eliminated, and the nutrients get into the bloodstream quickly, in a flood. The body has to take emergency action, releasing a great deal of insulin to digest the sugar. While this may be all right occasionally, there is growing evidence to suggest that repeatedly straining the body in this way can upset the delicate mechanism that controls the flow of insulin, resulting in diabetes. (Although not yet proved conclusively, the facts are pointing strongly in this direction.)

Finally, of course, lack of fiber means that when the food passes through the digestive tract, there is nothing to hold the water and provide the spongelike action. Without the softening, water-holding properties of fiber, waste matter is dry and hard and more difficult to move along the intestine. It tends to break up and get stuck in pockets along the way. This is one of the chief causes of diverticular disease, from which one in three people over the age of sixty suffer in the affluent countries. Hard, dry waste matter also takes longer to pass through the bowel, which can lead to constipation. Some experts think that when the passage of fecal matter through the bowel is slow, toxins may be reabsorbed by the body and that this may be linked with the increase in cancer of the bowel in the industrialized countries.

Thus fiber is a vital element in a healthy diet. Foods high in fiber are legumes (including baked beans); all fruits and vegetables, but in particular carrots and apples, because of the capacity of the fiber in these to reabsorb water; nuts and seeds; and whole grains, such as whole wheat, brown rice, and millet. These are the foods that normally feature prominently in a vegetarian/vegan diet, which is usually more than adequate from the point of view of fiber. The only time when a vegetarian or vegan diet may be low in fiber is if it is based on processed convenience foods; white flour, pasta, and rice; and dairy products. A diet like this could also be lacking important vitamins, but can easily be improved by swapping white bread, rice, and pasta for their whole-grain counterparts; by having whole wheat cereal or fruit, yogurt, and wheat germ for breakfast; by including more fresh fruits and vegetables, starting with, perhaps, salad sandwiches or a large salad for lunch and a good serving of green vegetables (cooked or as a salad) as part of the evening meal. A healthy diet should contain 35–50 grams of fiber each day. In table 2 are some examples of fiber in vegetarian foods:

TABLE 2 SOURCES OF FIBER		
FOOD	**WEIGHT**	**FIBER (IN GRAMS)**
¼ cup almonds	1⅓ ounces	1.0
1 medium-size apple	5 ounces	2.1
Dried apricots	1 ounce	6.8
Baked beans in tomato sauce	8 ounces	16.5
1 banana	6 ounces	3.4
1 cup bran flakes (breakfast cereal)	1 ounce	3.6
Brazil nuts	1 ounce	2.5
1 cup broccoli	5 ounces	5.75
1 large carrot	3½ ounces	3.0
5 figs	3½ ounces	18.4
4 mushrooms, sautéed	3½ ounces	2.45
1 cup rolled oats, raw	1½ ounces	3.0
¼ cup chopped parsley	9/10 ounce	0.2

TABLE 2 SOURCES OF FIBER		
FOOD	**WEIGHT**	**FIBER (IN GRAMS)**
¼ cup peanuts	1⅓ ounces	1.0
1 medium-size baked potato, eaten with skin	7 ounces	5.0
¼ cup (packed) raisins	1⅖ ounces	0.3
½ cup cooked red kidney beans	3½ ounces	7.9
½ cup cooked brown rice	3 ounces	1.8
2 slices whole-grain bread	1½ ounces	0.8

FAT

This question of fat is tied up with that of fiber, because if you think of fat in its most natural form, it is contained within the kernel of grains, nuts, and seeds, or bound up with some fiber in vegetables and fruits, such as the avocado. These are polyunsaturated fats and are essential to health; they are necessary for the absorption of the fat-soluble vitamins—A, D, E, and K. Of course we also add fat to our food in the form of milk, butter, egg yolk, margarine, and vegetable oils, and most people in developed countries eat far more fat than is needed. Calories from fat often make up about 40 percent of total calorie intake, whereas the ideal would be nearer 10 percent! This is a very difficult level to reach and would mean rather sparse meals of the kind most of us probably don't want to eat. Nonetheless, most of us can cut our fat intake a little, with beneficial results, by using a skim or semiskim milk in place of ordinary milk, using skim-milk yogurt and low-fat cheeses, and cutting down on the amount of fat we put on bread.

Some of the vegetarian sources of protein, such as cheese, nuts, and seeds, are quite high in fat but they are also concentrated sources of important nutrients and are used in small quantities: 1 to 2 ounces of nuts is an average serving, and is usually eaten along with fruit, legumes, or vegetables, which contain no fat. However, we vegetarians do need to be careful that we don't take too much fat through the overgenerous use of dairy products. Cheddar-type cheeses, for instance, are high in fat (the reduced-fat ones are recommended), but they are also concentrated, so 1½ to 2 ounces makes a generous serving. Compare this with the amount of meat that would make a satisfactory portion. Because of this, and the other valuable nutrients contained in cheese, it is an important food for lactovegetarians.

Regarding the type of fat one should use, and whether butter is

TABLE 3 PERCENTAGE OF FAT IN COMMON FOODS	
FOOD	**PERCENTAGE OF FAT**
Vegetable oils	100
Butter, margarine	85
Nuts	50–60
Heavy cream	50
Potato chips	37
Cheddar cheese	35
Chocolate	35
Piecrust dough	30
Sausage	30
Ground beef, pork, or lamb	20–30
Pound cake	25
Edam cheese	23
Plain biscuits	20
Sour cream, light cream	20
Oily fish	18
Avocado, soybeans	17
Eggs	12
Lean beef	10
French fries, wheat germ	9
Oats	8
Chicken	7
Whole milk, cottage cheese	4
Bread	1.5–3
Rice, pasta	1
Baked beans	0.5
White fish	0.5
Fruit, vegetables, all legumes except soybeans	0

preferable to margarine, I believe that the most important thing is to cut one's consumption of all fats, whether they are added to foods or eaten "hidden" in cakes and pastries. My own preference is for unsalted butter, used sparingly at the table and in some cooking. I recommend a good quality cold-pressed olive oil for all frying and cold-pressed corn, safflower, or soy oil on salads because of its high vitamin E content (see page 29). However, for deep frying it is necessary to use a good quality corn or sunflower that is not cold-pressed (though ideally deep frying should be kept to a minimum in a healthy diet). Vegans, of course, would use a good quality (preferably unsalted) polyunsaturated margarine instead of butter.

The reason for my choice of fats is that when vegetable oils are heated, as happens during the refining process and in the making of margarine, the chemical structure of the molecules is altered, and the valuable cis fatty acids, which the body needs, are altered and become trans fatty acids, which are harmful to health. There appears to be a link between high intake of trans fatty acids and some cancers, just as there appears to be a link between high intake of saturated fat and heart disease. Forewarned is forearmed! Butter and olive oil, on the other hand, are chemically more stable when heated, so I prefer to use them for cooking.

However, I must stress again that the most important thing is to reduce your overall fat intake. This does not mean giving up delicious dishes such as quiche or strawberries and cream; it just means planning for them. If you know you're going to have a dish that's high in fat in the evening, have cereal and fruit with skim milk for breakfast and a simple salad with whole-grain bread and low-fat red kidney beans or cottage cheese for lunch. Serve your quiche with steamed vegetables dressed with lemon juice and lots of chopped herbs, and a fresh fruit pudding, such as peaches in a raspberry puree, for dessert. That way you can have your fat and, hopefully, stay slim and healthy!

VITAMINS

Vitamins are substances that are essential for good health; a deficiency can result in a number of minor ailments and impaired health and growth, especially in children. The vitamins fall into two groups, those that are soluble in fat and can be stored in the body and those that are soluble in water.

Water-Soluble Vitamins

The water-soluble vitamins comprise the B vitamin complex and vitamin C. Because they dissolve in water, they have to be taken daily and can easily be lost or destroyed through contact with air, sunlight, heat, and water.

B Vitamins

There are thirteen B vitamins, and these are grouped together because they're interdependent. They tend to occur together in the same foods, and with the exception of B_{12}, you shouldn't take a supplement of an individual B vitamin, except under medical supervision, as this can upset the delicate balance.

Although we can get enough of these vitamins from nonanimal sources, it does mean eating good servings of green vegetables and whole grains. There is, however, a very concentrated source of all the B vitamins (except B_{12}), and that is brewers' yeast. Just one tablespoon of this (or the equivalent weight in brewers' yeast tablets) every day, plus a vegetarian or vegan diet planned along the lines described on pages 42–46, will ensure that your need for B vitamins is fully met. If for any reason you are allergic to wheat and thus not eating whole-grain bread (which is also a major source of B vitamins), you can cover your needs by taking an extra tablespoon of yeast, and basing your diet on fruits, vegetables, and one or two servings of other grains such as millet, together with regular servings of legumes and some dairy product if you eat this.

Vitamin B_1 — Thiamine
Thiamine is needed by the body for the release of energy from starch and sugar. A deficiency of this vitamin causes poor appetite and general lack of well-being. The best sources of thiamine are brewers' yeast, yeast extract, wheat germ, fortified breakfast cereals, and Brazil nuts and peanuts (both raw and roasted, although raw ones contain more thiamine). Oatmeal, millet, whole-grain bread, legumes, and peas are also good sources, and green vegetables, dried fruits, and (for

lactovegetarians) milk, yogurt, and cheese supply useful amounts. A vegetarian or vegan diet planned along the lines suggested in this book should contain more than enough thiamine to meet daily requirements.

TABLE 4
BEST VEGETARIAN/VEGAN SOURCES OF THIAMINE
(RDA: Average man, 1.4 mg; average woman, 1.0 mg; pregnant woman, 1.4 mg; lactating woman, 1.5; child up to age 5, 0.9 mg)

FOOD	WEIGHT	THIAMINE (IN MG)
2 slices whole-grain bread	1½ ounces	0.12
¼ cup raw millet	2 ounces	0.4
1 cup rolled oats, raw	1½ ounces	0.2
½ cup brown rice, cooked	3 ounces	0.07
⅔ cup whole wheat pasta, raw	2 ounces	0.6
1 cup fortified wheat flakes	1 ounce	0.35
¼ cup wheat germ, raw	9/10 ounce	0.5
½ cup cooked lentils or beans	3½ ounces	0.02
1 cup lentil sprouts, raw	3½ ounces	0.02
½ cup full-fat soy flour	1¼ ounces	0.2
1 cup soy milk	8 ounces	2.4
1 piece tofu	3½ ounces	0.06
1 egg	2 ounces	0.05
1 cup low-fat yogurt	8 ounces	0.1
1 cup low-fat milk	9 ounces	0.095
1 cup evaporated milk	9 ounces	0.118
Hard cheese	1½ ounces	0.01
¼ cup Brazil nuts	1⅓ ounces	0.3
¼ cup peanuts	1⅓ ounces	0.1*
1 tablespoon peanut butter	½ ounce	0.02
¼ cup walnuts	9/10 ounce	0.08
10 medium-size dates, pitted	3½ ounces	0.07
5 medium-size dried figs	3½ ounces	0.10
1 cup dried prunes	6¼ ounces	0.14
1 cup prune juice	8 ounces	0.03
¼ cup (packed) raisins	1⅖ ounces	0.04

TABLE 4
BEST VEGETARIAN/VEGAN SOURCES OF THIAMINE
(RDA: Average man, 1.4 mg; average woman, 1.0 mg; pregnant
woman, 1.4 mg; lactating woman, 1.5; child up to age 5, 0.9 mg)

FOOD	WEIGHT	THIAMINE (IN MG)
½ avocado	3½ ounces	0.10
1 banana	7½ ounces	0.08
1 cup cooked broccoli or sprouts	5 ounces	0.1
1 medium-size potato, baked in skin	7½ ounces	0.15
1 cup watercress	1½ ounces	0.03
1 tablespoon brewers' yeast	⅓ ounce	1.25
1 teaspoon yeast extract	⅕ ounce	0.25

*Up to 75 percent may be lost during roasting.

Vitamin B₂ (Riboflavin)

Like thiamine, riboflavin is needed for the release of energy from food, as well as for the absorption of iron. It is necessary for the proper functioning of the brain and resistance to infection. A lack of riboflavin can cause poor appetite and sores at the corners of the mouth and nose. Best sources are brewers' yeast, yeast extract, wheat germ, milk, and milk products. Millet, whole wheat pasta and fortified breakfast cereals, eggs, leafy green vegetables, and mushrooms also contain reasonable amounts. Other vegetables, whole-grain bread and oats, and fresh and dried fruits all contribute to the day's total. Most people get a high percentage of their riboflavin from milk and milk products; vegans, and vegetarians who are only eating small quantities of dairy products, need to monitor their intake of this vitamin. A daily spoonful of brewers' yeast (or the equivalent in yeast tablets, see page 43), and meals such as those described on pages 42–46, with a good serving each day of dark green leafy vegetables, plus moderate use of whole grains, peas and beans, and whole-grain bread and wheat germ (or extra yeast if you're allergic to these; see page 15), will ensure adequate amounts. If you're using soy milk, choose one that is fortified with riboflavin.

TABLE 5
BEST VEGETARIAN/VEGAN SOURCES OF RIBOFLAVIN
(RDA: Average man, 1.6 mg; average woman, 1.2 mg;
pregnant woman, 1.5 mg; lactating woman, 1.7 mg; child up to
age 5, 1.0 mg)

FOOD	WEIGHT	RIBOFLAVIN (IN MG)
2 slices whole-grain bread	1½ ounces	0.04
¼ cup raw millet	2 ounces	0.2
1 cup rolled oats, raw	1½ ounces	0.04
½ cup brown rice, cooked	3 ounces	0.15
⅔ cup whole wheat pasta, raw	2 ounces	0.42
1 cup fortified wheat flakes	1 ounce	0.42
¼ cup wheat germ, raw	9/10 ounce	0.2
½ cup cooked lentils or beans	3½ ounces	0.06
1 cup lentil sprouts, raw	3½ ounces	0.06
1 cup fortified soy milk	8 ounces	0.06
1 piece tofu	3½ ounces	0.03
1 egg	2 ounces	0.15
1 cup low-fat yogurt	8 ounces	0.49
1 cup low-fat milk	9 ounces	0.40
1 cup evaporated milk	9 ounces	0.79
Hard cheese	1½ ounces	0.16
¼ cup peanuts, without skins	1⅓ ounces	0.05
1 tablespoon peanut butter	½ ounce	0.02
¼ cup walnuts, without skins	9/10 ounce	0.05
½ avocado	3½ ounces	0.10
1 banana	7½ ounces	0.14
1 cup cooked broccoli	5 ounces	0.31
4 medium-size mushrooms, sautéed	2½ ounces	0.27
1 medium-size potato, baked in skin	7½ ounces	0.07
1 tablespoon brewers' yeast	⅓ ounce	0.34
1 teaspoon yeast extract	⅕ ounce	0.34

Niacin

Niacin has a function similar to that of riboflavin, and a deficiency can cause similar symptoms, including mouth ulcers. It is found in brewers' yeast and yeast extract; wheat germ; whole-grain bread; whole grains, especially millet and whole wheat pasta; legumes; cheese; avocados; dried apricots, dates, and figs; vegetables, especially mushrooms, dark green leafy vegetables, and asparagus; and almonds and walnuts. Peanuts are one of the richest sources of all: Two ounces of roasted peanuts (without skins), or ½ cup peanut butter, supplies 75 percent of the recommended daily allowance for a woman! Although whole-grain cereals are a good source of niacin, it is not certain how much of this is available to the body, because it is in a bound form. However, by taking brewers' yeast and, including frequent servings of the foods mentioned above, it is possible to meet the recommended levels. In a survey of vegan mothers in the United Kingdom, levels of niacin were found to be well above average, probably because of the prominence of legumes and yeast extracts in their diet.

TABLE 6 BEST VEGETARIAN/VEGAN SOURCES OF NIACIN (RDA: Average man, 18 mg; average woman, 13 mg; pregnant woman, 15 mg; lactating woman, 18 mg; child up to age 5, 11 mg)		
FOOD	**WEIGHT**	**NIACIN (IN MG)**
2 slices whole-grain bread	1½ ounces	1.2
¼ cup raw millet	2 ounces	1.31
1 cup rolled oats, raw	1½ ounces	0.4
½ cup brown rice, cooked	3 ounces	4.6
⅔ cup whole wheat pasta, raw	2 ounces	4.0
1 cup fortified wheat flakes	1 ounce	3.5
¼ cup wheat germ, raw	9/10 ounce	1.05
½ cup cooked lentils or beans	3½ ounces	2.5
1 cup lentil sprouts, raw	3½ ounces	1.1
½ cup full-fat soy flour	1¼ ounces	0.72
1 cup soy milk	8 ounces	0.5
1 piece tofu	3½ ounces	0.05

TABLE 6
BEST VEGETARIAN/VEGAN SOURCES OF NIACIN
(RDA: Average man, 18 mg; average woman, 13 mg; pregnant
woman, 15 mg; lactating woman, 18 mg; child up to age 5, 11
mg)

FOOD	WEIGHT	NIACIN (IN MG)
1 cup low-fat yogurt	8 ounces	0.26
1 cup low-fat milk	9 ounces	0.21
1 cup evaporated milk	9 ounces	0.49
Hard cheese	1½ ounces	0.03
¼ cup almonds, skinned	1⅓ ounces	1.25
¼ cup peanuts, skinned, roasted	1⅓ ounces	6.15
1 tablespoon peanut butter	½ ounce	2.4
¼ cup sunflower seeds	1⅓ ounces	1.95
¼ cup sesame seeds	1⅓ ounces	0.85
¼ cup walnuts	9/10 ounce	0.22
1 cup dried apricots or peaches	4¼ ounces	3.0
10 medium-size dates, pitted	3½ ounces	2.0
5 medium-size dried figs	3½ ounces	1.7
1 cup dried prunes	6¼ ounces	2.6
1 cup prune juice	8 ounces	1.0
Raisins	1⅖ ounces	0.03
5–6 asparagus, cooked	3½ ounces	0.8
⅔ cup fava beans, cooked	3½ ounces	3.0
½ avocado	3½ ounces	1.0
1 banana	7½ ounces	1.2
1 cup cooked broccoli or sprouts	5 ounces	1.2
4 mushrooms, sautéed	2½ ounces	2.9
1 medium-size potato, baked in skin	7½ ounces	2.4
⅔ cup peas, cooked	3½ ounces	1.0
⅔ cup rutabagas, raw grated, lightly packed	3½ ounces	1.2
⅔ cup rutabagas, cooked	3½ ounces	0.8
1 tablespoon brewers' yeast	⅓ ounce	3.0

Pantothenic Acid

Pantothenic acid is found in all foods except for fats, sugar, and spirits, and is needed for the release of energy and for the proper functioning of the adrenal glands. A deficiency of this vitamin can lead to the development of allergies and may cause excessive tiredness, sensations of pins and needles, restlessness, and stomach cramps. Canning and processing of food can destroy 30 to 75 percent of the pantothenic acid in foods. No RDAs have been given for this vitamin, and the best sources of it are the same as for the other B vitamins (brewers' yeast, yeast extract, eggs, peanuts, wheat germ, mushrooms, whole-grain bread and cereals, cheese, and legumes), so so if you are getting enough of the other B vitamins, you are probably getting enough pantothenic acid as well.

Vitamin B₆ (Pyridoxine)

This vitamin is needed for the metabolism of protein and for the formation of blood. Lack of vitamin B_6 can result in irritability, depression, sore mouth, and skin and scalp irritation, and may contribute to heart disease and diabetes. Best sources are brewers' yeast, yeast extract, and wheat germ; whole-grain bread, whole grains, and fortified breakfast cereals; legumes and sprouted legumes; nuts, especially Brazil nuts and walnuts; dark green leafy vegetables; corn; cabbage; avocado; and dried and fresh fruits, especially banana and

TABLE 7 BEST VEGETARIAN/VEGAN SOURCES OF PYRIDOXINE (B₆) (RDA: Average man, 2.2 mg; average woman, 2.0 mg; pregnant woman, 2.6 mg; lactating woman, 2.5 mg; child up to age 5, 1.3 mg)		
FOOD	WEIGHT	PYRIDOXINE (IN MG)
2 slices whole-grain bread	1½ ounces	0.08
1 cup rolled oats, raw	1½ ounces	0.04
1 cup fortified wheat flakes	1 ounce	0.08
¼ cup wheat germ, raw	9/10 ounce	0.23

TABLE 7
BEST VEGETARIAN/VEGAN SOURCES OF PYRIDOXINE
(B$_6$)
(RDA: Average man, 2.2 mg; average woman, 2.0 mg;
pregnant woman, 2.6 mg; lactating woman, 2.5 mg; child up to
age 5, 1.3 mg)

FOOD	WEIGHT	PYRIDOXINE (IN MG)
½ cup cooked lentils or beans	3½ ounces	0.30
1 egg	2 ounces	0.68
1 cup low-fat yogurt	8 ounces	0.11
1 cup low-fat milk	9 ounces	0.10
1 cup evaporated milk	9 ounces	0.13
Hard cheese	1½ ounces	0.03
¼ cup Brazil nuts	1⅓ ounces	0.05
¼ cup walnuts	9/10 ounce	0.18
10 medium-size dates, pitted	3½ ounces	0.10
5 medium-size dried figs	3½ ounces	0.32
1 cup dried prunes	6¼ ounces	0.44
½ avocado	3½ ounces	0.42
1 banana	7½ ounces	0.40
1 cup corn, cooked	6 ounces	0.47
9 medium Brussels sprouts, raw	3½ ounces	0.28
1 medium-size potato, baked in skin	7½ ounces	0.40
1 tablespoon brewers' yeast	⅓ ounce	0.20

pineapple. Vitamin B$_6$ is also found in eggs, milk, and milk products. A diet planned along the lines described on pages 42–46 will meet the requirements of this vitamin. When vegetables are boiled, this vitamin leaches out into the cooking water, but the loss of this nutrient can be avoided by using just enough water to be absorbed during the cooking, or by straining off and reusing the cooking water, or by using other methods of cooking, such as stir frying, or by serving fruits and vegetables raw.

Folic Acid

Folic acid is used by the body, along with vitamin B$_{12}$, for cell division, and a deficiency may cause a form of anemia. All foods except fats, sugar, and spirits contain some folic acid, but for vegetarians the

TABLE 8 BEST VEGETARIAN/VEGAN SOURCES OF FOLIC ACID (RDA: Average man, 400 mcg; average woman, 400 mcg; pregnant woman, 800 mcg; lactating woman, 500 mcg; child up to age 5, 200 mcg)		
FOOD	**WEIGHT**	**FOLIC ACID (IN MCG)**
2 slices whole-grain bread	1½ ounces	42
1 cup rolled oats, raw	1½ ounces	140
¼ cup wheat germ, raw	9/10 ounce	66
½ cup cooked lentils or beans	3½ ounces	168
1 cup lentil sprouts, raw	3½ ounces	12
½ cup full-fat soy flour	1¼ ounces	311
1 egg	2 ounces	36*
1 cup low-fat yogurt	8 ounces	17
1 cup low-fat milk	9 ounces	12
1 cup evaporated milk	9 ounces	20
¼ cup almonds	1⅓ ounces	13
¼ cup walnuts	9/10 ounce	21.6
1 banana	7½ ounces	20
10 medium-size dates, pitted	3½ ounces	25
5 medium-size dried figs	3½ ounces	30
1 orange	6 ounces	40
½ avocado	3½ ounces	10
1 cup cooked broccoli or sprouts	5 ounces	50–70
1 medium-size potato, baked in skin	7½ ounces	15
1 cup watercress	1½ ounces	17.5
1 tablespoon brewers' yeast	⅓ ounce	192

*Only half of this may be available if cooked.

richest sources are brewers' yeast, yeast extract, and wheat germ. Whole-grain bread and whole grains are also valuable sources, as are most vegetables (especially dark green leafy ones, asparagus, and sprouted legumes) and fruits (especially oranges and bananas). Nuts (especially walnuts and almonds) and pumpkin seeds are also good sources. For lactovegetarians, cheese, milk, and eggs also contribute. Folic acid is sensitive to heat and light, and 50 to 90 percent of the folic acid in vegetables can be destroyed by cooking, so serve plenty of salads; stir fry or cook vegetables carefully for as short a time as possible in the smallest quantity of water, and save the water for use in soups and sauces. Some brewers' yeast and wheat germ each day, together with the grains, fresh vegetables, legumes, fruits, and nuts that make up a balanced vegetarian or vegan diet, will ensure sufficient amounts of this vitamin.

Vitamin B_{12}

Vitamin B_{12} functions similarly to vitamins B_1, B_2, and niacin, but in addition it is needed for the production of bone marrow. A deficiency

---

TABLE 9
BEST VEGETARIAN/VEGAN SOURCES OF VITAMIN B_{12}
(RDA: Average man, 3 mcg; average woman, 3 mcg; pregnant woman, 4 mcg; lactating woman, 4 mcg; child up to age 5, 2–3 mcg)

FOOD	WEIGHT	VITAMIN B_{12} (IN MCG)
1 cup soy milk, fortified with B_{12}	8 ounces	4.07*
1 egg	2 ounces	0.39
1 cup low-fat yogurt	8 ounces	1.28
1 cup low-fat milk	9 ounces	3.0
1 cup evaporated milk	9 ounces	0.61
Hard cheese	1½ ounces	0.8
1 teaspoon yeast extract	⅕ ounce	0.41
1 cup fortified breakfast cereal	1 ounce	0.5

*This varies from brand to brand, so check the one you use.

can cause pernicious anemia. The major source of B_{12} is meat and dairy products; the vitamin is almost entirely absent from plants. Therefore, vegetarians, and especially vegans, need to pay particular attention to alternative sources in their diet. Vegetarians can get some B_{12} from eggs and dairy products, and some brewers' yeast is fortified with B_{12}, as are most yeast extracts, some breakfast cereals, and some soy milks (read the labels), but vegetarians and vegans who are not getting much from these sources would be well advised to take a supplement.

Vitamin C

Vitamin C is important for resistance to infection and is needed for the absorption of iron, tissue repair, and normal growth. Vitamin C

TABLE 10 BEST VEGETARIAN/VEGAN SOURCES OF VITAMIN C (RDA: Average man, 60 mg; average woman, 60 mg; pregnant woman, 80 mg; lactating woman, 100 mg; child up to age 5, 45 mg)		
FOOD	WEIGHT	VITAMIN C (IN MG)
1 cup lentil sprouts, raw	3½ ounces	14
4 asparagus spears, cooked	3½ ounces	26
½ avocado	3½ ounces	14
1 banana	7½ ounces	15
1 cup cooked broccoli	5 ounces	140
¼ cantaloupe	3½ ounces	33
½ medium-size grapefruit	3½ ounces	38
1 orange	6 ounces	66
1 cup orange juice	9 ounces	124
½ cup sliced red pepper	2 ounces	102
1 medium-size potato, baked in skin	7½ ounces	16
1 cup strawberries	5 ounces	88
1 medium-size tangerine	4 ounces	27
1 medium-size tomato	5 ounces	34
1 cup watercress	1½ ounces	28

is present in many fresh fruits and vegetables, but it is easily lost through exposure to air, heat, and water. However, a normal vegetarian or vegan diet, with its abundance of fruits and vegetables, is unlikely to be lacking in vitamin C. One-half cup of orange juice supplies daily needs, and raw cabbage, cauliflower, watercress, and tomatoes are other good sources. Cooked cabbage and potatoes also contain useful amounts.

Fat-Soluble Vitamins

Vitamins A, D, E, and K dissolve in fat. They can therefore be stored in the body. Vitamins A and D can be toxic in high doses, so supplements should only be taken at the recommended levels.

Vitamin A

There a two forms of this vitamin, one that is found in dairy products and fortified margarine and another, called beta-carotene, that is

TABLE 11 BEST VEGETARIAN/VEGAN SOURCES OF VITAMIN A (RDA: Average man, 5,000 IU; average woman, 4,000 IU; pregnant woman, 5,000 IU; lactating woman, 6,000 IU; child up to age 5, 2,500 IU)		
FOOD	**WEIGHT**	**VITAMIN A (IN IU)**
1 cup dried apricots	4½ ounces	14,170
3 average-size fresh apricots	4 ounces	2,890
4 spears asparagus, cooked	3½ ounces	900
1 average-size banana	5¼ ounces	270
1 cup cooked broccoli	5½ ounces	3,800
¼ cantaloupe	3½ ounces	3,400
1 large carrot, raw	3½ ounces	11,000
1 orange	6½ ounces	260
1 cup orange juice	9 ounces	500
1 medium-size peach	4 ounces	1,330
1 medium-size tangerine	4 ounces	360
1 medium-size tomato	5¼ ounces	1,350
1 cup watercress	1¼ ounces	1,720

TABLE 11
BEST VEGETARIAN/VEGAN SOURCES OF VITAMIN A
(RDA: Average man, 5,000 IU; average woman, 4,000 IU;
pregnant woman, 5,000 IU; lactating woman, 6,000 IU; child
up to age 5, 2,500 IU)

FOOD	WEIGHT	VITAMIN A (IN IU)
1 ounce Cheddar cheese	1 ounce	300
2 tablespoons butter or margarine	1 ounce	940
1 egg	2 ounces	590
1 cup low-fat milk*	9 ounces	150
1 cup whole milk	9 ounces	279

*Enriched.

found in many dark green, orange, and yellow fruits and vegetables. Beta carotene is converted into vitamin A by the body. Vitamin A is essential for the proper functioning of the eyes and for the mucous membranes throughout the body, also for proper growth and resistance to infection. A deficiency increases the risk of infections in the throat, eyes, and skin, also bronchitis. Vitamin A is found in spinach and other dark green leafy vegetables and in orange fruits and vegetables, especially carrots, 3 ounces of which more than supply the day's requirements. Other good sources are butter, eggs, cheese, and fortified margarines. A normal vegetarian or vegan diet is not likely to be short of this vitamin.

Vitamin D
The body needs vitamin D in order to use calcium efficiently. This vitamin is present in few foods, and with the exception of margarine and some breakfast cereals (which are fortified with vitamin D), they are all animal products. The richest source is cod liver oil, which is obviously unsuitable for both vegetarians and vegans, also eggs, butter, milk (including evaporated and fortified skim—check the label), cheese, yogurt, and cottage cheese. Vegetarian and vegan sources of vitamin D are given in table 12, and it is easy to check whether your

TABLE 12
VEGETARIAN/VEGAN SOURCES OF VITAMIN D
(RDA: Average man, 5 mcg; average woman, 5 mcg; pregnant woman, 10 mcg; lactating woman, 10 mcg; child up to age 5, 10 mcg)

FOOD	WEIGHT	VITAMIN D (IN MCG)
2 tablespoons butter	1 ounce	0.42
2 tablespoons margarine	1 ounce	2.24
1⅓ cups low-fat cottage cheese, not packed	10 ounces	0.06
1 cup low-fat yogurt	8 ounces	0.045
1 cup low-fat milk	9 ounces	0.11
1 cup evaporated milk	9 ounces	6.52
Hard cheese	1½ ounces	0.08
1 egg	2 ounces	0.75

normal diet is supplying enough vitamin D to meet the recommended levels.

Vitamin D is also created by the action of sunlight on the skin, but unless you live in a very sunny part of the world and do a lot of sunbathing, it's best not to rely on this source. People with dark skins cannot absorb vitamin D from sunshine, so they can become deficient in vitamin D. Many experts recommend a daily vitamin D supplement for everyone, whether vegetarian or not, and I think this is sensible advice, especially for young children and old people. But if you are taking any general vitamin tablets, check whether these contain vitamin D before adding any extra to your diet; and if you're taking a vitamin D supplement, be careful to measure the dose precisely, because excessive vitamin D is toxic.

Vitamin E

Vitamin E improves general vitality and is important for the functioning of the heart. It may help to avoid atherosclerosis (hardening of the arteries) and high blood pressure. It is also said to increase fertility, help prevent varicose veins, and improve the body's ability to heal itself. The best sources of vitamin E are wheat germ; cold-pressed

TABLE 13
BEST VEGETARIAN/VEGAN SOURCES OF VITAMIN E
(RDA: Average man, 10 mg; average woman, 8 mg; pregnant
woman, 10 mg; lactating woman, 11 mg; child up to age 5,
6 mg)

FOOD	WEIGHT	VITAMIN E (IN MG)
1 tablespoon cold-pressed corn oil	½ ounce	11.0*
1 tablespoon wheat germ oil	½ ounce	21.5*
2 slices whole-grain bread	1½ ounces	1.0
¼ cup almonds	1⅓ ounce	4.2
¼ cup wheat germ	9/10 ounce	3.0
1 cup cooked Brussels sprouts	5 ounces	1.0

*Compare with olive oil, which is 0.7 mg for same amount.

vegetable oils, especially corn, safflower, and wheat germ oil; almonds; peanuts; and Brazil nuts. Eggs, butter, cheese, whole wheat flour and bread, oats, rice, and millet are also quite good sources, as are apples, bananas, cantaloupe, oranges and grapefruit. A vegetarian diet, with its regular use of whole grains, nuts, and seeds, is unlikely to be short of this vitamin (see table B, "How It All Adds Up," in the Appendix).

Vitamin K
Necessary for blood clotting and to prevent excess loss of blood after injury, vitamin K can be manufactured by the intestinal bacteria, except when the process is inhibited as a result of taking antibiotics. (Consuming active yogurt or acidophilus culture afterward will help restore the intestinal bacteria so that they can do their job.) Vitamin K is found in leafy green vegetables, tomatoes, soybean oil, egg yolks, and seaweed. A daily serving of leafy green vegetables will make sure that you have an adequate amount of this vitamin.

MINERALS

There are fifteen minerals that are essential for the health of the body, and five more that are thought to be necessary. The most important of these are iron, calcium, magnesium, phosphorus, potassium, and sodium.

Iron

Iron is needed for the formation of blood and for carrying oxygen in the blood; lack of iron can cause anemia. In a vegetarian diet, iron is obtained from legumes (soybeans and lentils are excellent sources); soy flour and whole-grain cereals, especially whole-grain bread and millet (which contains the most iron of the grains); nuts and seeds; dark green vegetables; and dried fruits (apricots and prunes are particularly good sources). Brewers' yeast, molasses, and wheat germ are concentrated sources of iron, and egg yolk is a useful source, too, for vegetarians eating dairy products. A vegetarian or vegan diet that is planned along the lines suggested on pages 42–46 will meet the recommended iron levels. As demonstrated in the analysis on pages 244–45, it should include several slices of whole-grain bread daily, along with a serving of legumes or sprouts, a couple of servings of grains such as millet, whole-grain pasta, or oatmeal (or the equivalent in extra slices of whole-grain bread), a few nuts and seeds (especially almonds, cashews, Brazil nuts, and pumpkin seeds), a little dried fruit, and a serving of dark green leafy vegetables among other fruits and vegetables.

Not all the iron in food can be used by the body, since other components in the diet prevent it from being absorbed, and the RDA is set high to make allowance for this. In this respect, vegetarians and vegans do have a problem because many of our iron-rich foods, such as nuts, wheat, peas, and beans, also contain a substance called phytic acid, which combines with iron (and other minerals, such as zinc) and prevents full absorption. This effect is lessened when iron-rich foods are eaten along with a source of vitamin C, such as orange juice. So when you make bread, use the vitamin C method (see page 220), which includes ascorbic acid among the ingredients. And if you buy it, choose bread that has risen in preference to soda breads, since well-risen whole-grain bread contains less phytic acid, and that is further broken down in the baking process. In addition, usual processes of soaking, sprouting, and cooking legumes help to break down phytic acid, as does the soaking of oatmeal overnight for breakfast muesli. It is helpful to know that blanched almonds and skinned peanuts contain less phytic acid than those with the skins on. And since it's the bran in whole-grain flour that contains most of the phytic acid, it's best not to add extra bran to your meals, except under medical supervision. In fact, this really shouldn't be necessary under normal conditions because a vegetarian diet is naturally high in fiber.

Fortunately, research has shown that after a time the body adapts to a vegetarian diet, so that phytic acid is digested lower down in the intestine, after minerals such as iron and zinc have been absorbed. Apparently, this adaptation is accomplished quickly, and if you are already eating some high-fiber foods, such as whole-grain bread, your body is most likely already making the change.

If you're worried about your iron level, choose an iron-rich grain

---

TABLE 14
BEST VEGETARIAN/VEGAN SOURCES OF IRON
(RDA: Average man, 10 mg; average woman, 18 mg; pregnant/lactating woman, no figures given, since average U.S. diet considered unable to meet requirements and iron supplements given routinely [but U.K. figure only 15 mg, and 18 mg when not pregnant!]; child up to age 5, 15 mg)

FOOD	WEIGHT	IRON (IN MG)
2 slices whole-grain bread	1½ ounces	1.0
¼ cup raw millet	2 ounces	3.9
1 cup rolled oats, raw	1½ ounces	1.7
½ cup rolled oats, cooked	4 ounces	0.7
½ cup brown rice, cooked	3 ounces	0.4
⅔ cup whole wheat pasta, raw	2 ounces	5.4
1 cup enriched pasta, cooked	5 ounces	1.3
1 cup fortified wheat flakes	1 ounce	2.0
¼ cup wheat germ, raw	9/10 ounce	2.3
½ cup cooked lentils or beans	3½ ounces	2–3.0
1 cup lentil sprouts, raw	3½ ounces	3.0
½ cup cooked soybeans	3¼ ounces	2.5
½ cup full-fat soy flour	1¼ ounces	3.0
1 cup soy milk	8 ounces	1.8
1 piece tofu	3½ ounces	1.9

TABLE 14
BEST VEGETARIAN/VEGAN SOURCES OF IRON
(RDA: Average man, 10 mg; average woman, 18 mg;
pregnant/lactating woman, no figures given, since average U.S.
diet considered unable to meet requirements and iron
supplements given routinely [but U.K. figure only 15 mg, and
18 mg when not pregnant!]; child up to age 5, 15 mg)

FOOD	WEIGHT	IRON (IN MG)
1 egg	2 ounces	1.4
¼ cup almonds	1⅓ ounces	1.7
¼ cup Brazil nuts	1⅓ ounces	1.2
¼ cup peanuts	1⅓ ounces	0.8
1 tablespoon peanut butter	½ ounce	0.3
¼ cup pumpkin seeds	1⅓ ounces	3.9
¼ cup sesame seeds	1⅓ ounces	0.9
¼ cup sunflower seeds	1⅓ ounces	2.6
1 cup dried apricots or peaches	4¼ ounces	7.2
10 medium-size dates, pitted	3½ ounces	3.0
5 medium-size dried figs	3½ ounces	3.0
1 cup dried prunes	6¼ ounces	6.3
1 cup prune juice	8 ounces	10.5
¼ cup (packed) raisins	1⅖ ounces	1.4
½ avocado	3½ ounces	1.5
1 banana	7½ ounces	0.5
1 cup cooked beet greens	5 ounces	2.8
1 cup cooked broccoli or sprouts	5 ounces	1.2–1.7
¼ cup chopped parsley	⁹⁄₁₀ ounce	0.9
1 medium-size potato, baked in skin	7½ ounces	1.1
1 cup cooked spinach	6 ounces	4.0
1 cup raw spinach	2 ounces	1.7
1 tablespoon tomato puree	½ ounce	1.0
1 cup cooked vegetables	5 ounces	1.0
1 cup watercress	1½ ounces	0.7
1 tablespoon blackstrap molasses	¾ ounce	3.2
1 tablespoon brewers' yeast	⅓ ounce	1.4

such as millet or whole-grain pasta in preference to rice; almonds, preferably blanched; and pumpkin seeds. Concentrate on the legumes that are highest in iron—lentils and soybeans—either cooked or sprouted. Have nibbles of dried fruit, add a little soy flour to your cooking where possible, and take the suggested supplement of brewers' yeast each day. You can also boost your iron level by taking some blackstrap molasses daily, right from the spoon if you like the flavor, dissolved in milk, or mixed with a little honey. You can also drink prune juice, which is much more palatable than it sounds (especially with a shot of soda water!), or use it to moisten your breakfast cereal (it's good with muesli) or to soak dried fruits to make a compote.

Calcium

Calcium is needed for the health of bones, skin, and teeth and for the function of the heart. It is also involved in bloodclotting. The richest sources of calcium are milk, cheese, and yogurt, and it's not difficult for lactovegetarians to obtain enough from these sources. Even a vegetarian eating a diet that is fairly low in dairy products, with just, say, one cup of milk or ¾ cup yogurt during the day, can easily reach the RDA by including, for instance, a cup of cooked broccoli and a few dried figs, which are good sources. Vegans would be well advised to use a calcium-enriched soy milk for drinking and making yogurt and to include a calcium-rich green leafy vegetable and some figs in their diet daily if possible. These foods, together with the grains, whole-grain bread, nuts, fruits, legumes, and vegetables that make up the day's meals should ensure that needs are met. It's surprising, too, how much you can increase your calcium intake by small garnishes and nibbles: One-half ounce parsley scattered over a meal adds 15 mg of calcium; 1 ounce sesame seeds adds 31 mg; ¼ cup flaked almonds, 83 mg. Calcium is a mineral that needs watching in the vegan diet. In a survey of vegan mothers in England the calcium levels of some were found to be on the low side. If you're worried about your calcium level, an easy way to increase this is to make your own bread and add 1 teaspoon of calcium carbonate (prepared chalk) to each pound flour. You could also consider taking calcium tablets. (Check both these suggestions with your obstetrician if you're pregnant.)

TABLE 15
BEST VEGETARIAN/VEGAN SOURCES OF CALCIUM
(RDA: Average man, 800 mg; average woman, 800 mg;
pregnant/lactating woman, 1,200 mg; child up to age 5,
540–800 mg)

FOOD	WEIGHT	CALCIUM (IN MG)
2 slices whole-grain bread	1½ ounces	46
¼ cup raw millet	2 ounces	12
1 cup rolled oats, raw	1½ ounces	23
½ cup rolled oats, cooked	4 ounces	11
½ cup brown rice, cooked	3 ounces	9
Whole wheat pasta, raw	2 ounces	144
¼ cup wheat germ, raw	9/10 ounce	18
½ cup cooked lentils or beans	3½ ounces	25
1 cup lentil sprouts, raw	3½ ounces	12
½ cup cooked soy beans	3¼ ounces	65
½ cup full-fat soy flour	1¼ ounces	70
1 cup soy milk	8 ounces	48
1 piece tofu	3½ ounces	128
Vegan cheese (see page 138)	2 ounces	77
1⅓ cups low-fat cottage cheese, not packed	10 ounces	200
1 cup low-fat yogurt	8 ounces	415
1 cup low-fat milk	9 ounces	302
¼ cup skim-milk powder	½ ounce	302
Hard cheese	1½ ounces	315
1 egg	2 ounces	27
¼ cup almonds	1⅓ ounces	83
¼ cup Brazil nuts	1⅓ ounces	65
¼ cup peanuts	1⅓ ounces	26
1 tablespoon peanut butter	½ ounce	11
¼ cup pumpkin seeds	1⅓ ounces	18
Sesame seeds	1 ounce	31
Sunflower seeds	1 ounce	34
1 tablespoon tahini	½ ounce	15

TABLE 15 BEST VEGETARIAN/VEGAN SOURCES OF CALCIUM (RDA: Average man, 800 mg; average woman, 800 mg; pregnant/lactating woman, 1,200 mg; child up to age 5, 540–800 mg)		
FOOD	WEIGHT	CALCIUM (IN MG)
1 cup dried apricots or peaches	4¼ ounces	87
10 medium-size dates, pitted	3½ ounces	59
5 medium-size dried figs	3½ ounces	126
1 cup dried prunes	6¼ ounces	82
1 cup prune juice	8 ounces	36
¼ cup (packed) raisins	1⅖ ounces	25
½ avocado	3½ ounces	20
1 banana	5 ounces	12
1 cup cooked beet greens	5 ounces	144
1 cup cooked broccoli	5 ounces	136
1 cup raw cabbage	3 ounces	34
1 large carrot, raw	3½ ounces	37
¼ cup chopped parsley	9/10 ounce	30
1 medium-size potato, baked in skin	7½ ounces	14
1 cup cooked spinach	6 ounces	167
1 cup raw spinach	2 ounces	51
1 cup watercress	1½ ounces	53
1 tablespoon blackstrap molasses	¾ ounce	137
1 tablespoon light molasses	¾ ounce	33
1 tablespoon raw sugar	½ ounce	7
1 tablespoon brewers' yeast	⅓ ounce	17
1 tablespoon carob powder	¼ ounce	28

Phosphorus

Phosphorus is needed, together with calcium, for the formation and health of teeth and bones. It is present in many foods: milk, eggs, cereals, nuts, fruits, and vegetables, and there is no problem for either vegans or vegetarians in getting enough of this mineral.

Magnesium

Magnesium is needed for healthy bones and teeth and also for the process of drawing energy from carbohydrate foods. The best sources of magnesium for vegetarians and vegans are almonds, Brazil nuts, wheat germ, and peanuts; soy flour and soybeans, millet, and oatmeal. There is also some in dried and fresh fruit and in leafy green vegetables, and some in whole wheat bread, which, in a balanced diet all adds up over the course of the day to more than the recommended daily level. However, this is another mineral that is affected by the presence of phytic acid, as I explained on pages 30–31. Water-soluble, magnesium may be lost if you throw away the cooking water from boiled vegetables, although it is not damaged by heat, so that fried, grilled, and baked vegetables retain their full amount. A normal vegetarian or vegan diet should provide plentiful supplies of this mineral.

TABLE 16
BEST VEGETARIAN/VEGAN SOURCES OF MAGNESIUM
(RDA: Average man, 350 mg; average woman, 300 mg;
pregnant/lactating woman, 450 mg; child up to age 5, 200 mg)

FOOD	WEIGHT	MAGNESIUM (IN MG)
2 slices whole-grain bread	1½ ounces	36
¼ cup raw millet	2 ounces	92.25
1 cup rolled oats, raw	1½ ounces	38
½ cup rolled oats, cooked	4 ounces	25
½ cup brown rice, cooked	3 ounces	45
1 cup enriched pasta, cooked	5 ounces	27
¼ cup wheat germ, raw	9/10 ounce	84
½ cup full-fat soy flour	1¼ ounces	90
1 piece tofu	3½ ounces	111
¼ cup almonds	1⅓ ounces	96
¼ cup Brazil nuts	1⅓ ounces	88
¼ cup peanuts	1⅓ ounces	63
1 tablespoon peanut butter	½ ounce	26
¼ cup sesame seeds	1⅓ ounces	87
¼ cup sunflower seeds	1⅓ ounces	14
1 tablespoon tahini	½ ounce	25

TABLE 16
BEST VEGETARIAN/VEGAN SOURCES OF MAGNESIUM
(RDA: Average man, 350 mg; average woman, 300 mg;
pregnant/lactating woman, 450 mg; child up to age 5, 200 mg)

FOOD	WEIGHT	MAGNESIUM (IN MG)
1 cup dried apricots or peaches	4¼ ounces	81
10 medium-size dates, pitted	3½ ounces	58
5 medium-size dried figs	3½ ounces	71
1 cup dried prunes	6¼ ounces	74
1 cup prune juice	8 ounces	26
¼ cup (packed) raisins	1⅖ ounces	14
1 cup cooked beet greens	5 ounces	2.8
1 cup cooked broccoli or sprouts	5 ounces	1.2–1.7
¼ cup chopped parsley	⁹⁄₁₀ ounce	6
1 medium-size potato, baked in skin	7½ ounces	1.1
1 cup cooked spinach	6 ounces	4.0
1 cup raw spinach	2 ounces	1.7
1 cup watercress	1½ ounces	0.6
1 tablespoon blackstrap molasses	¾ ounce	3.2
1 tablespoon brewers' yeast	⅓ ounce	19
1 tablespoon carob powder	¼ ounce	0.3

Potassium and Sodium

Potassium and sodium together control the fluid balance throughout the organs and tissues of the body. The ratio of potassium to sodium is higher in the muscles, organs, and soft tissues of the body, whereas sodium predominates in the blood plasma and interstitial fluids. The better each of these minerals predominates in its own area, the better our health is likely to be. Both sodium and potassium occur naturally in foods, but we also add sodium to our diet in the form of salt. For this reason, and because the foods rich in potassium are fresh raw fruit and vegetables, which do not figure prominently in many people's diet, most people have too much sodium and too little potassium. This means that gradually the proper sodium-potassium balance in their body breaks down, and all the vital organs, especially the liver and heart, can eventually suffer. Too little potassium can also contribute to tiredness, because potassium helps in the process of carrying oxygen to the cells.

A vegetarian diet is usually high in potassium because of the fresh fruits and vegetables it normally contains. There is also potassium in wheat germ, legumes, and whole grains, so there is no problem in obtaining enough of this mineral. You can further improve your diet by being sparing in your use of salt to season foods and by avoiding buying salty manufactured foods.

TRACE ELEMENTS

Trace elements are substances known to be present in the body and to be used in conjunction with other minerals and vitamins. Research into their subtle interaction with other substances and their function and importance is continuing, but a deficiency has been noted in a variety of physical and mental disorders.

Zinc

Zinc is vitally important in the formation of DNA and RDA (the hereditary material of all organisms). A deficiency of zinc often manifests as white flecks on the fingernails and skin problems, such as eczma and acne. You should make a point of including in your diet foods that are rich in this mineral. The best sources of zinc for vegetarians are wheat germ and bran, but these contain phytic acid, which can prevent some absorption (see pages 30–31). Other good sources are brewer's yeast, whole-grain bread and other grains, and nuts and seeds, especially pumpkin seeds. Legumes, either cooked or sprouted; green leafy vegetables, especially spinach; corn; peas; mushrooms; fresh asparagus; and mango are also good sources. Cheese, milk, and yogurt can supply useful amounts for lactovegetarians. Although consumption of this trace element needs watching, a vegetarian diet containing some milk and cheese will probably meet the requirements. If you're vegan, make sure that you're using a good quality soy milk that contains zinc, and be sure to include other zinc-rich foods.

Zinc absorption appears to be linked to the amount of iron in the diet, so taking iron supplements or a large quantity of quickly absorbed iron, as in some meats, can mean that more zinc is needed. Fortunately, iron obtained from fibrous foods, such as legumes, cereals, nuts, and fruits does not have this disadvantage, and a vegetarian or vegan may not therefore require the high levels of zinc sometimes suggested. Nature does have a way of making things balance!

TABLE 17
BEST VEGETARIAN/VEGAN SOURCES OF ZINC
(RDA: Average man, 15 mg; average woman, 15 mg; pregnant woman, 20 mg; lactating woman, 25 mg; child up to age 5, 10 mg)

FOOD	WEIGHT	ZINC (IN MG)
2 slices whole-grain bread	1½ ounces	1.0
1 cup rolled oats, raw	1½ ounces	0.6
½ cup brown rice, cooked	3 ounces	0.4
1 cup fortified wheat flakes	1 ounce	0.7
¼ cup wheat germ, raw	9/10 ounce	3.6
½ cup cooked lentils or beans	3½ ounces	1.0
1 cup lentil sprouts, raw	3½ ounces	1.6
1 cup soy milk	8 ounces	.5
Cheddar cheese	1½ ounces	1.25
Gouda cheese	1½ ounces	1.58
1 cup cottage cheese, not packed	8 ounces	0.95
1 cup low-fat milk	9 ounces	0.95
1 cup low-fat yogurt	8 ounces	2.02
1 egg	2 ounces	0.84
¼ cup almonds, roasted	1⅓ ounces	1.0*
¼ cup Brazil nuts	1⅓ ounces	1.8
¼ cup cashews, roasted	1⅓ ounces	1.5*

TABLE 17
BEST VEGETARIAN/VEGAN SOURCES OF ZINC
(RDA: Average man, 15 mg; average woman, 15 mg; pregnant
woman, 20 mg; lactating woman, 25 mg; child up to age 5, 10
mg)

FOOD	WEIGHT	ZINC (IN MG)
1 mango, raw	11 ounces	1.41
1 orange	6 ounces	0.26
¼ cup (packed) raisins	1⅖ ounces	0.07
1 cup cut asparagus pieces, raw	4½ ounces	1.31
½ avocado	3½ ounces	0.35
1 cup cooked broccoli	5 ounces	0.23
1 cup cooked Brussels sprouts	5 ounces	0.54
1 cup raw cauliflower	3½ ounces	0.37
1 cup raw mushrooms	2½ ounces	0.91
1 cup cooked peas	5½ ounces	1.2
1 medium-size potato, baked in skin	7½ ounces	0.6
1 cup cooked spinach	6 ounces	1.3
1 cup cooked corn	5½ ounces	0.7
1 tablespoon brewers' yeast	⅓ ounce	.44

*Raw nuts may contain more.

Manganese

Another vitally important trace element, manganese is abundant in
nuts, peas and beans, and whole grains but the phytic acid that is also
present in these foods interferes with its absorption to some degree,
although how much is not yet known. The best sources are whole-
grain bread, wheat germ, almonds, Brazil nuts, cashews, peanuts, and
walnuts. Dried figs, dates, peaches, and apricots are also good sources,
and brewers' yeast also supplies some. Potatoes, bananas, and fresh
fruit and vegetables generally also contribute. A vegetarian or vegan
diet planned along the lines suggested should not be deficient in this
mineral.

Iodine

Iodine is necessary for the proper functioning of the thyroid gland. The main sources are seafoods (including seaweeds and thus vegetarian jelling agents, such as agar and gelose), and iodized table salt. For vegetarians and vegans, a good way of making sure you're getting enough iodine is to add a pinch of kelp powder to food two or three times a week, take kelp tablets regularly, add a little dried seaweed to stocks, or crumble or snip soaked or, in the case of nori, crisped seaweed over salads and vegetable stir-fries.

For an at-a-glance table of these nutrients and the best sources in the diet, please see table A, "Summary of Nutrients," in the Appendix.

Creating a
Balanced Diet

If you've read this far and you're feeling quite confused by all the dietary requirements and their various possible sources, I don't blame you! It does seem complicated, yet it can be simplified. Here is a basic eating plan that supplies the recommended daily allowances of nutrients. Base each day's meals around the following foods.

Basic Foods for a Day's
Healthy Vegetarian or Vegan Meals

- *4 slices whole-grain bread*
- *2 servings of other cereals,* such as 1 cup cooked millet or rice, 2 ounces (dry weight) whole wheat pasta, 1 cup raw rolled oats, 1 cup enriched whole wheat breakfast cereal, or 2 additional slices of whole-grain bread
- *2 heaping tablespoons wheat germ*
- *2 servings of protein foods,* such as ½ cup sprouted legumes; ½ cup tofu; some hard cheese, cottage cheese, or yogurt; or a serving of nuts, peanut butter, or pumpkin seeds
- *1½ cups milk or calcium-fortified soy milk, or 1 cup yogurt*
- *1 cup cooked (or ¾ cup raw) green leafy vegetables*
- *A source of vitamin C,* such as ½ cup orange juice, ½ cantaloupe, 2 tomatoes, ¾ cup raw cabbage, ½ green pepper, ¾ cup strawberries, 1 orange, or ½ grapefruit
- *A little dried fruit*
- *A few nuts and seeds,* especially almonds, peanuts, or pumpkin seeds; also Brazil nuts, walnuts, cashews, or sunflower or sesame seeds
- *1 tablespoon brewers' yeast,* or, if you're allergic to wheat, you can replace the bread and wheat germ with an extra tablespoon brewers' yeast
- *A little butter or margarine* for vitamin A PLUS fruits, vegetables,

and dairy products as desired PLUS vitamins B$_{12}$ and D and iodine supplements as necessary

The extra fruits, vegetables, nuts, and dairy products you add to this basic framework enable you to make daily menus that are as sumptuous or as thrifty as you like. The menus on pages 44–45 are an example.

Incidentally, if you find the idea of taking brewers' yeast difficult to contemplate, try stirring a little into fruit juice or whizzing it up into the banana drink on page 96 (which is the most palatable way I've found of taking it). You can also try it sprinkled over breakfast cereal. It is such an excellent food, providing a B-vitamin "safety net," that it's well worthwhile to experiment until you find a brand of brewers' yeast you can tolerate and a way of taking it. Yeast tablets are an alternative: buy those that are made of pure brewers' yeast and take enough to equal one tablespoon of the powder (8 g); thus, with 300 mg tablets, you'd take 25 of them.

As you may have noticed, many of the same foods crop up time and again as good sources of nutrients. I call these the five-star foods because of the useful quantities they contain of various nutrients. So when you're choosing additional foods to fill out your basic diet, you might like to bear the following in mind.

Five-Star Foods
- Dried fruits, especially figs; also prunes and prune juice, apricots, peaches, dates
- Nuts and seeds, especially almonds, Brazil nuts, cashews, walnuts, peanuts, and pumpkin, sunflower, and sesame seeds
- Potatoes, carrots, parsley, broccoli, cabbage, Brussels sprouts, rutabagas, cauliflower, mushrooms, corn, peas, fava beans, asparagus, okra, avocado, bananas, oranges, mangos
- Molasses, carob, yeast extract

Here is how you could use the basic foods to create a day's meal plan:

> 1½ cups milk or soy milk (used throughout the day in drinks, on cereals, and so forth)

ONE WEEK'S VEGETARIAN/VEGAN MENUS
(Should include 1 to 2 cups low-fat or fortified soy milk)

	BREAKFAST	LUNCH	DINNER
Day 1	Grated apple and plain yogurt with raisins, 2 tablespoons wheat germ, and sprinkling of sunflower seeds Whole-grain toast	Lentil Soup Vitality Salad Bowl Whole-grain bread or roll	Easy Cauliflower Cheese Spinach Carrots Muesli, Oaty Version
Day 2	½ grapefruit Whole wheat flakes with raisins and milk or soy milk Whole-grain toast	Salad sandwiches on whole-grain bread Roasted peanuts Banana	Chili red beans served on brown rice with corn Green salad Dried-Fruit Compote or soaked apricots with natural yogurt or tofu topping and wheat germ
Day 3	Orange juice Muesli with raisins, nuts, wheat germ and milk or soy milk Whole-grain toast	Soybean Salad in pita bread or with whole-grain bread Pear	Stir-fried Vegetables Brown rice with toasted almonds and sunflower seeds Real-fruit yogurt
Day 4	½ cantaloupe Whole-grain toast	Greek Salad with pita bread	Spicy Lentils and Potatoes

	BREAKFAST	LUNCH	DINNER
ONE WEEK'S VEGETARIAN/VEGAN MENUS (Should include 1 to 2 cups low-fat or fortified soy milk)			
		Peaches with yogurt, wheat germ, and chopped almonds	Stir-fried broccoli with ginger Muesli, Original Version
Day 5	Oatmeal with a few raisins (sprinkle with wheat germ, or add it to evening loaf)	Tabbouleh with pita bread Orange or sliced oranges with toasted slivered almonds	Soy and Walnut Loaf with applesauce Cooked green vegetable Fresh tomato sauce Baked potato Carob Pudding
Day 6	Muesli with wheat germ and chopped fresh fruit, such as strawberries or banana Whole-grain toast	Beet, Orange, and Cottage Cheese Salad Whole-grain roll Apple Sunflower seeds and dates	Millet Pilaf with Mixed Vegetables Avocado, Watercress, and Walnut Salad Tofu Ice Cream
Day 7	Fresh grapefruit sections Yogurt with chopped dried fruit and wheat germ Whole-grain toast	Hummus with pita bread and some raw vegetable crudités, such as red pepper strips, carrot, cauliflower, scallions, and celery Nuts, dates, and figs	Broccoli vinaigrette Whole wheat Pasta Rings with Tomato Sauce Grated cheese or toasted pumpkin and sunflower seeds Fresh fruit

Breakfast

Muesli made from:
    1 cup rolled oats
    2 tablespoons wheat germ
    2 to 3 chopped figs or dates
    1 ounce slivered almonds
    1 ounce pumpkin seeds
    1 slice whole-grain toast

OR 1 cup enriched whole wheat breakfast cereal

Lunch

Sandwiches made from:
    3 to 4 slices whole-grain bread, yeast extract, and cheese or peanut butter
Tomato
Orange
Nuts, seeds, and dried fruit

Dinner

Lima bean and vegetable casserole
Brown rice or crusty whole-grain garlic bread
Green salad or cooked Brussels sprouts
Fresh fruit or baked apple

Snacks

Whole-grain toast with honey, yeast extract, or peanut butter
Fresh fruit
Carrot or celery sticks or raw cauliflower
Nuts and raisins
Cheese cubes

For an analysis that shows how the day's meal plan described above meets daily nutritional requirements, see table B, "How It All Adds Up," in the Appendix.

Dietary Changes in Preparation for Pregnancy

A vegetarian or vegan diet, planned along the lines suggested, will supply you with the basic nutrients you need for health and vitality. If you are improving your health in preparation for becoming pregnant in the future, it is strongly recommended that you change to some form of contraception other than the pill. The pill is known to affect the body's ability to metabolize vitamins B_6, B_2, B_{12}, and folic acid, as well as zinc, copper, and iron. Make sure your intake of vitamins B_{12} and D is adequate (see pages 24, 28); take supplements if necessary.

Also especially monitor your levels of the other B vitamins and take the daily dietary supplement of brewers' yeast or its equivalent in yeast tablets. Make sure you're getting enough vitamin E and iron and as often as possible include the zinc-rich foods: pumpkin seeds, fresh mango, corn, almonds, asparagus, and sprouted legumes. Use a seaweed-vegetable stock (see pages 101–2) for iodine and other trace minerals or add a pinch of powdered kelp to your food several times a week.

Relax and be happy!

Diet for Pregnancy and Breast-feeding

During pregnancy, your daily nutrient requirements increase considerably, as is shown in table C, "Recommended Daily Dietary Allowances for Women," in the Appendix on pages 246–47. More iron is needed to allow for the growing baby and to enable your body to make more blood, which may be increased by as much as 30 percent. Your need for folic acid is doubled, and you also need more of all the other B vitamins as well as vitamins A, C, D, and E. Your calcium requirement increases by around 50 percent. Your requirements during breast-feeding are similar, but with even more need for vitamins A, C, E, thiamine, riboflavin, niacin, iodine, and zinc; you will also require a little less extra protein and B_6, and much less extra folic acid.

In order to meet these needs, any diet, no matter whether it is vegetarian, vegan, or one that includes meat and fish, has to be enriched with extra nutrients. Table 18 shows the additions that have to be made to a vegetarian or vegan diet to bring the daily nutrients up to the required level.

An easy way to ensure you're getting enough of the very valuable and important B vitamins is to take an extra 2 tablespoons brewers' yeast each day. This will automatically take care of the extra thiamine, riboflavin, niacin, B_6, and folic acid needed during both pregnancy and lactation, while adding only 46 calories and providing a useful extra 2.8 mg of iron, some zinc, and a little calcium and magnesium, too. The vegetarian/vegan diet already supplies enough vitamin E, but you could boost your total further by using an additional 2 teaspoons cold-pressed corn, safflower, or soy oil to dress salads or vegetables.

Vegetarian and vegan diets are naturally rich in vitamins A and C, but you can make sure that you're covered here by having an extra orange or half cup of orange juice, a large banana, a piece of cantaloupe, or an extra serving of green vegetables.

The additional calcium requirement is most easily met by taking an extra 1½ cups of skim milk or calcium-fortified soy milk, 1 cup of yogurt, or 2 ounces of hard cheese.

If you take the additional brewers' yeast, this will more than cover your increased phosphorus requirements and will contribute 38 mg of magnesium. The milk or soy milk adds about another 40 mg of magnesium, the banana or orange around 50 mg. This comes to 128 mg, and the remaining 22 mg can easily be made up by having a few dates, a couple of dried figs, a few raisins and nuts, or a piece of whole-grain bread. Or you could cover your magnesium need completely by having 2 extra tablespoons of wheat germ, which also contributes nearly 3 mg toward the extra zinc needed, and together with the yeast (another 0.9 mg), the milk or soy milk (1.43 mg), and the banana or orange juice (0.3 mg), goes a long way toward meeting the extra need for zinc during pregnancy. You will need to boost this level even more when you're breast-feeding, so try to include some other rich sources each day, such as pumpkin seeds, extra soy sprouts, Brazil nuts, and, if the budget permits, asparagus or fresh mango.

These suggestions automatically increase both your iron and your protein intake as follows:

TABLE 18 HOW TO INCREASE YOUR DAY'S PROTEIN AND IRON			
FOOD	WEIGHT	IRON (IN MG)	PROTEIN (IN G)
2 tablespoons brewers' yeast	⅔ ounce	2.8	6.2
1½ cups soy milk	12 ounces	2.7	12.0
1½ cups skim milk	13 ounces	0.18	12.8
1 banana	6 ounces	1.0	1.6
2 tablespoons wheat germ	⅔ ounce	1.9	5.6
Pumpkin seeds	1 ounce	3.1	8.12
Total with soy milk		11.5	33.52
Total with skim milk		8.98	34.32

The protein more than meets the extra suggested for pregnancy (30 g) and lactation (20 g). No official levels have been set for the daily intake of iron during pregnancy and lactation, since the Food and Nutrition Board of the National Academy of Sciences states, "The increased requirement during pregnancy cannot be met by the iron content of typical American diets nor by existing stores of many women; therefore, the use of 30 to 60 mg of supplemental iron is recommended." Your obstetrician will no doubt advise you on this matter, but the additional iron supplied by the foods just mentioned will certainly be helpful. Ask your obstetrician also about extra vitamin D and iodine.

SUGGESTIONS FOR WAYS TO INCLUDE THE EXTRA FOODS IN YOUR DIET

These nutrient-rich foods can of course be added to your meals or you can have them in the form of snacks, which is often more helpful when you're pregnant.

One of the best ways to take brewers' yeast is in a soothing, sustaining drink. To make this, whizz in the blender 1 cup of milk, 2 tablespoons yogurt, brewers' yeast, and 1 banana. You can also add the recommended extra oil, unless you want to use it in something else during the day. The rest of the yogurt can be made into a kind of muesli, with the wheat germ, some raisins, chopped dates, or figs, a few pumpkin seeds or almonds, and perhaps a chopped apple. If you feel like extra snacks during the day, try whole-grain toast with yeast extract, peanut butter, or honey; pumpkin seeds, raisins, and dates; fresh peaches or mango.

Alternatively you could stir the brewers' yeast into some orange or tomato juice. Try whizzing some of the yogurt with a little peeled cucumber, some garlic, walnuts, and the oil to make a chilled soup, or with a fresh peeled mango to make a delectable drink, and eat the rest of the yogurt with wheat germ and raisins. Another delicious and irresistible snack, if you feel like something sweet but healthy, is the Nutty Carob Bananas on page 233; try coating them with wheat germ for an extra treat.

TO AVOID DURING PREGNANCY

Alcohol

Heavy intake of alcohol (especially early on in pregnancy) has been linked with some birth defects. Pregnant mothers have always been warned not to drink more than a glass or two of wine occasionally, but medical opinion now suggests that it's safest to avoid alcohol altogether during pregnancy.

Smoking

Smoking during pregnancy is associated with low birth weight and, again, medical opinion cautions seriously against it. Unlike most things, smoking has a worse effect later in pregnancy than in the first few weeks. So it's never too late to cut down or give up smoking.

Medication

Medication of any kind should be considered very carefully and certainly only taken when prescribed by a doctor who knows about your pregnancy. This applies also to vitamin supplements. In animal studies, massive doses of vitamin D have resulted in birth defects. And large doses of vitamin C have been shown to condition the fetus to require more than normal, so that after birth the baby may develop scurvy. The usual iron supplement recommended by the Food and Nutrition Board of the National Academy of Sciences is 30 to 60 mg, but this, too, should be taken only under medical supervision.

COPING WITH POSSIBLE PROBLEMS IN PREGNANCY

Morning Sickness

When you first become pregnant, you may well feel slightly sick and not much like eating. During these early days you may find that there are only certain things you want to have. Some people find milk, milky drinks, and yogurt helpful, while others turn to fresh fruits, salads, or whole-grain bread. Herb teas, especially peppermint, linden, and chamomile (see page 100), can be useful.

For most people this stage only lasts for the first few weeks. If you do find you cannot eat normally, do not fear that your baby is being undernourished. Only if you are constantly sick and cannot keep anything down should you see your doctor, for in that case the baby could be at risk. Otherwise, just try to make sure that the foods you do eat are as whole and as natural as possible.

Once you know what is happening, you will probably find that you can control the nausea to some extent by having something to eat or drink as soon as you feel that strange, hungry, sick feeling. It is often helpful to avoid fatty foods and to eat little and often. Dry whole-grain toast or crackers might be helpful. You might also try eating a few dates or drink a little apple or orange juice.

Food Cravings

The tendency to have odd cravings for foods in pregnancy is well known, and, within reason, these do not usually do any harm. If excessive, they may show a lack of some mineral, particularly iron (take medical advice), but minor food cravings are normal and, in my opinion, are to be indulged if possible, for they'll pass as the pregnancy progresses.

Heartburn

If you are suffering from heartburn (usually caused by the growing baby pressing against your stomach), it may help if you eat frequent small meals and cut out fatty foods as much as possible. Also avoid eating concentrated starches (potatoes, bread, brown rice, and other grains) at the same time as you eat concentrated protein (cheese, eggs, dairy products). Plan for a starch meal, which can include nuts and seeds and all the fresh vegetables you want, plus the "starchy" fruits (dates, dried fruit, bananas, and grapes); and a protein meal, which should be based on protein, nuts and seeds, and all kinds of vegetables (except potatoes) and fruits (except the starchy ones just mentioned, though raisins are all right). Legumes, since they are a half-and-half protein-carbohydrate mix in their natural state, need sprouting before use, at which point they can go with either meal.

Constipation

A tendency toward constipation can be helped by the inclusion in your diet of foods that are high in fiber: whole-grain bread, legumes, nuts, fresh vegetables (including potatoes), and fruits (especially raspberries). If you are also suffering from hemorrhoids, try to include buckwheat in your diet as often as possible, since this food contains rutin, a natural remedy for hemorrhoids and also for varicose veins.

Excessive Weight Gain

A close check will be kept on your weight during your pregnancy. There is no reason why a vegetarian diet should be any more fattening than a conventional one, but pregnancy is a time when many women find they gain extra pounds very easily. If you find that your weight is increasing too rapidly, you would be wise to concentrate on the low-calorie high-protein foods, such as cottage and farmer cheese, yogurt, tofu, legumes, wheat germ, and skim milk, with liberal amounts of fresh vegetables and fruit.

However, some people are now questioning the wisdom of restricting weight gain too drastically during pregnancy. I rather go along with this view. Some reserves of fat (but not too many!) are helpful when it comes to the demands upon your body of breast-feeding; they can also help you weather the general stresses and strains of the early days with a young baby. And if you breast-feed for at least six months, you will almost certainly find that this extra weight just melts away even though you are, quite rightly, eating more than normal. But you do have to be patient while your food stores, in the form of body fat, are gradually used up in the production of milk for the baby. Then, with any luck, you'll find you're thinner and more gorgeous than ever. But if not, then when breast-feeding is over is the time to restrict your calories to around 1,000 or 1,200 a day in order to get back your slim figure.

Thinking Ahead about Food and Meals

Few people who haven't had the experience of living with a young baby can have any idea of how completely and utterly this tiny addition to the family can disrupt life! So if this is your first experience, take it from me, life will never be the same again, and unhurried preparation of delicious suppers for two will definitely be a thing of the past, at least for the first few weeks or months. So, it is not being overly cautious to plan out some menus now, perhaps along the lines of those on pages 59–63, getting the appropriate dishes safely stashed away in the freezer! In fact, the more complete meals you can get into the freezer before the baby is born, the better. All the dishes in the freezer section, pages 140–64, freeze well. In addition, it's helpful to have some of the following "freezer basics" for making vegetarian/vegan meals quickly and easily:

- *Cooked Beans.* A supply of your favorite varieties, frozen in convenient quantities, is most useful and saves having to rely on cans when you're in a hurry. Varieties that I find particularly useful are red kidney beans, lima beans, chick-peas, and soybeans. Prepare a 1-pound bag at a time. Wash the beans, then soak them for 6 to 8 hours in cold water. Drain the beans into a colander and rinse under cold water. Then put the beans into a pot with fresh cold water. Sometimes, especially with soybeans, I add 6 to 8 bay leaves. Bring to a boil and boil hard for 10 minutes, then simmer gently until tender, about 1 hour for red kidney beans and lima beans, 2 to 3 hours for chick-peas, and 3 hours for soybeans.

You can save time and fuel by using a pressure cooker. Place the trivet in the base of the pressure cooker and put the beans into the metal basket or container. Add 2 cups water, bring to pressure, and cook for 15 minutes, or 1 hour for soybeans and chick-peas.

Whichever cooking method you use, drain the beans and divide them into approximately 10-ounce portions, which are each roughly equivalent to the drained contents of a 15-ounce can. Pack in suitable containers; I generally put mine into small plastic bags, then gather all these into another, larger one in order to keep them together. Label and freeze. Though it's best to thaw these before use, they can be used straight from the freezer if you put them into a colander and rinse under hot water to separate them.

• *Whole Wheat Bread Crumbs.* Very convenient as an addition to nut roasts and savory bakes, whole wheat bread crumbs are also frequently used for topping au gratin dishes and coating rissoles. To prepare them, remove the crusts from slices of bread, break the bread into pieces, and whizz it to crumbs in a food processor or blender. The bread needs to be on the stale side: I generally use up odd bits and pieces from the bread bin as they accumulate. Freeze in a plastic bag and use as required.

For dried bread crumbs, spread fresh crumbs in a thin layer on an ungreased baking sheet. Bake at 375°F for about 10 minutes, or until golden brown. Store in the freezer or in an airtight jar.

• *Chopped Parsley.* I find a bag of chopped parsley very useful indeed. Wash parsley well, remove the stalks, chop—this can be done speedily in a food processor—and store in the refrigerator or freezer in a plastic bag.

• *White Sauce.* Although white sauce can be made fairly quickly, it saves time and effort if you have some in the freezer for serving with nut savories and for adding to cooked vegetables and legumes for au gratin dishes. Prepare according to the recipe on page 140 and freeze in 1-cup containers.

• *Tomato Sauce.* Another indispensable basic. Follow the recipe on page 142 and freeze in 1-cup containers.

• *Vegetarian Gravy.* If you like gravy with nut savories, it's worth making up an extra-large batch and freezing it in 1-cup containers.

• *Whole Wheat Quiche Shells.* Although a quiche shell can be made quickly, again, it's handy to have some ready-baked ones in the freezer. They can be used straight from the freezer and quickly filled with an easy egg-and-cheese mixture or vegetables in a white or cheese sauce, then baked.

• *Prepared Dishes.* The most useful dishes to make for the freezer are ones that are complete in themselves (or with a sauce that you freeze with them) and need only a simple vegetable or salad to accompany them. Casserole dishes and vegetable, nut, or legume pies with potato or pastry toppings are examples. Nut roasts are useful, frozen either whole or in slices. It's especially helpful if you also freeze a sauce for serving with them.

STOCKING THE SHELVES

In addition to stocking the freezer, as your pregnancy draws to a close, you'll want to make sure that your cupboard and refrigerator are well stocked with some of the basics needed for making quick meals.

• *Eggs.* If you eat dairy products, eggs are a great natural convenience food. Scrambled eggs on whole wheat toast or a buttery-flavored omelet with a creamy inside make soothing and welcoming quick meals. Hard-boiled eggs are a useful way of adding protein to a rice or vegetable dish or can be combined with a cheese or parsley sauce to make a main dish in their own right.

• *Cheese.* Again, for vegetarians eating dairy products, cheese is a useful standby for quick meals, so it's worth grating up a good quantity to keep in the refrigerator for when you need it quickly. Vegan cheese, made from soy flour (page 138) can be used similarly, so it's worth making up a good quantity and keeping some in the freezer. Grilled cheese—grated cheese heaped on top of unbuttered whole wheat toast and melted under a broiler—makes an almost instant supper and is delicious with watercress or a sliced tomato and scallion salad, which can be quickly made while the cheese is melting. Cooked, easy-to-prepare vegetables such as cauliflower can be placed in a shallow, ovenproof dish, sprinkled with grated cheese, and grilled to make a protein-rich main dish (see page 188). And grated cheese will turn baked or mashed potatoes into a main course (for other, nondairy toppings for baked potatoes, see page 191).

• *Grains.* Some of the most popular grains are brown rice, millet, and bulgur, and they are all extremely easy to prepare (see recipe section). They provide a good basis for a main dish or turn a vegetable mixture such as ratatouille or even just a good homemade tomato or curry sauce into a complete meal. Grains are a good source of protein but can be made even better by adding small quantities of grated or cubed cheese; chopped hard-boiled egg; nuts; sunflower, pumpkin, or sesame seeds; or cooked red kidney beans, chick-peas, or lima beans. The mixture can be made tasty by adding some of the more quickly prepared vegetables, perhaps fried with some spices, before serving.

• *Legumes.* Cans of beans—or a supply of your own home-cooked beans in your freezer, frozen in convenient quantities, as described on page 54—are very useful for quick meals. Look for beans canned in just salt and water, without other additives if possible. Add them to vegetable stews; fork them into cooked brown rice; coat with a simple oil and vinegar dressing for a filling salad; or mix with a tasty sauce and serve with rice or millet, potato, crisp whole wheat toast, or just a simple salad.

Also in this category, since it's made from soy, is tofu, a nutritious bean curd that has been used in China for centuries. It looks rather like white cheese and has a bland flavor. You can buy either a soft or a firm version, vacuum-packed and refrigerated, from most supermarkets these days; they keep much longer than the fresh, unpackaged kind. The firm one is the most useful for dips, spreads, stir fries, and fritters, whereas the soft one is nice in creams and custards.

• *Split Red Lentils.* Lentils are especially useful because they cook, without presoaking, in 20 minutes. Use them to make a thick, nourishing soup (see page 105), which can make a filling meal if you serve it with whole wheat bread; or make them into a sauce to serve with whole wheat pasta (see page 176); or for the spicy potato-and-lentil mixture (see page 184) to serve with brown rice or sliced raw tomato and chutney.

• *Whole-Grain Flour.* I find that cooks are divided into those who find pastry making easy and think of a pie as a quick dish and those who consider it a real labor. If you come into the first group, it's worth-while to have a bag of self-raising 85 percent or 100 percent whole-grain flour in the refrigerator for making the quick quiches on pages 174 and 175. These can be served with just watercress or a simple green salad for a complete main course.

• *Nuts and Seeds.* Nuts and seeds provide instant protein for adding to dishes of cooked vegetables, salads, or grains in order to make them into a main course. Cashews are useful, as are almonds, pumpkin seeds (which are the richest in iron), and walnuts. Peanuts are cheap, nutritious (being especially rich in B vitamins), and tasty if you buy raw shelled ones and roast them yourself.

To roast peanuts, spread them out on a dry baking sheet and bake for about 15 minutes at 400°F. The nuts under the skins should be golden brown. Let cool, then store. You can rub off the skins, but I don't bother; it's the roasting that makes all the difference to the flavor. I prefer to buy hazelnuts in their skins from health food stores and roast them in the same way.

• *Vegetables.* Some vegetables require far less preparation than others, and these are the ones to choose when you're short of time. Potatoes can be just scrubbed and baked, and new potatoes only need scrubbing before boiling, thus conserving the valuable nutrients just under the skin in addition to saving time. Other easy vegetables are cauliflower and broccoli (both of which are especially nutritious), mushrooms, scallions, tomatoes, red and green peppers, and beets. Unless you choose the large ones, onions can be a bit of a nuisance to prepare, but they're desirable for flavor.

I also like to keep in the freezer some packets of "casserole vegetables" as a basis for quick stews, as well as one or two small packets of mixed vegetables for adding to cooked millet or rice, along with toasted slivered almonds, to make a pilaf (see page 173). Canned tomatoes are also indispensable. You might also want to focus on easy-to-use salad ingredients, such as large-leaf (therefore easy to wash) watercress, clean-looking lettuce and celery, and cucumber.

• *Whole Wheat Pasta.* Like the grains, this food can make a quick and healthy basis for a meal. I especially like whole wheat pasta rings, which seem lighter in texture than some of the other varieties. Serve it with a quickly made tomato sauce and grated cheese (or sunflower seeds or toasted slivered almonds) or with red pepper and lentil sauce (see page 176) or peanut and tomato sauce (see page 189).

Here is a sample menu for those precious days and nights just after the birth. They are based on nutritious foods and make use of freezer dishes (marked F) and quick dishes made from the other basics.

TWO WEEKS' EASY MENUS FOR THE EARLY DAYS AFTER THE BABY'S BIRTH		
	BREAKFAST **LUNCH** **DINNER**		

	BREAKFAST	LUNCH	DINNER
Day 1	Orange juice with a heaping teaspoon brewers' yeast Cereal with raisins and nuts	Lentil and Mushroom Spread Whole-grain toast Tomato Apple	Rice, Cheese, and Spinach Bake (save portion for next day's lunch) Carrots Banana with Carob Sauce
Day 2	Grated or chopped apple with plain yogurt, wheat germ, raisins Whole-grain toast (optional)	Rice, Cheese, and Spinach Bake (saved from previous night) Sliced tomatoes and scallions	Lima Bean and Vegetable Casserole Watercress or cooked green vegetable, such as broccoli, kale, or cabbage Grapes or crackers and a little cheese
Day 3	Dried apricots soaked overnight in orange or prune juice and topped with spoonful of plain yogurt and sprinkling of wheat germ Whole-grain toast (optional)	Sprouted Chick-pea Salad in Pita Bread Fresh fruit (optional)	Broccoli and Tomato au Gratin (F) (save some for next day's lunch) New potatoes Corn Carob Pudding (optional)

TWO WEEKS' EASY MENUS FOR THE EARLY DAYS AFTER THE BABY'S BIRTH			
	BREAKFAST	LUNCH	DINNER
Day 4	½ grapefruit Whole wheat cereal with raisins, wheat germ, and milk	Broccoli and Tomato au Gratin (saved from previous night), served hot or cold, as salad, with hard-boiled-egg wedges Crisp bread	Soy and Walnut Loaf (F) (save some for next day's lunch) Applesauce (F) Gravy (F) New potatoes, carrots Fruit compote with thick yogurt or tofu topping
Day 5	Orange juice Muesli with raisins, wheat germ, and milk Whole-grain toast (optional)	Soy and Walnut Loaf (saved from previous night) Beet, Apple, and Alfalfa Salad Yogurt Dressing	Broccoli Pilaf (F) with toasted almonds Chinese cabbage, Tomato, and Scallion Salad Apricot Fool with Sesame Topping (optional)
Day 6	½ cantaloupe Whole-grain toast	Quick Lentil Soup Watercress and tomato salad or sandwiches	Asparagus (or spinach or broccoli) Croustade (F) (save piece for lunch next day) Carrots Tomato salad Fresh fruit (optional)

TWO WEEKS' EASY MENUS FOR THE EARLY DAYS AFTER THE BABY'S BIRTH		
	BREAKFAST	**LUNCH**	**DINNER**
Day 7	Strawberries or banana topped with plain yogurt Whole-grain toast with honey	Asparagus Croustade (saved from previous night) Carrot, Apple and Chick-pea Salad	Millet Pilaf with Mixed Vegetables (F) Carrots and corn Green salad Fresh fruit
Day 8	Orange juice Whole wheat cereal with raisins and wheat germ Whole-grain toast (optional)	Salad sandwiches on whole-grain bread Fresh fruit	Tofu Fritters with Lemon Parsley Sauce Broccoli or Brussels sprouts Grilled tomatoes or tomato salad Strawberries
Day 9	Prunes or dried peaches soaked overnight in prune or orange juice and served with yogurt and wheat germ	Hummus and pita bread Fresh fruit	Broccoli in Cheese Sauce (F) (save some for next day's lunch) Carrot, Apple, and Mint Salad Carob and Cashew Squares
Day 10	Orange or grapefruit juice Whole wheat cereal with wheat germ and raisins Whole-grain toast (optional)	Broccoli in Cheese Sauce (saved from previous night) Tomato salad Nuts or sunflower seeds	Pasta with Lentil and Red Pepper Sauce Green salad Tangerines

TWO WEEKS' EASY MENUS FOR THE EARLY DAYS AFTER THE BABY'S BIRTH			
	BREAKFAST	LUNCH	DINNER
Day 11	Soaked dried apricots with plain yogurt, honey, and wheat germ Whole-grain toast (optional)	Watercress Soup (F) Whole wheat crisp breads with cottage cheese or Tofu Spread and a sprinkling of sesame seeds	Lentil Enchiladas (F) (save portion for next day's lunch) Tomato Sauce (F) Rice Green salad or cooked green leafy vegetable Peaches with almonds
Day 12	Orange or grapefruit sections Whole-grain toast with honey or yeast extract	Lentil Enchilada (saved from previous night) Cabbage, Apple, and Raisin Salad	Broccoli or Asparagus Croustade (F) (save portion for next day's lunch) Mashed potatoes Pear and Carob Tart
Day 13	Orange juice Whole wheat flakes with wheat germ and raisins Whole-grain toast (optional)	Broccoli or Asparagus Croustade (saved from previous night) Corn and radish salad Pear	Hummus with toast Alfalfa Slaw Nuts and raisins or stuffed fresh dates

TWO WEEKS' EASY MENUS FOR THE EARLY DAYS AFTER THE BABY'S BIRTH		
	BREAKFAST	**LUNCH**	**DINNER**
Day 14	Grapefruit juice Muesli with raisins, wheat germ, and milk Whole-grain toast	Mixed-Bean Salad with fresh lettuce or watercress Apple	Stir-fried Vegetables Brown rice Tofu Ice Cream

NOTES ON MENUS

• It is helpful to save a portion of the evening meal for your lunch the following day, either to reheat or to eat cold.

• It is assumed that you will take 3 cups of milk during the day, and that at least 1 cup of this will be used in drinks, on breakfast cereals, and in main dishes when applicable. If you are breast-feeding, you'll need to take another 3 to 4 cups, which can be taken as extra milky drinks or can be "swapped" with other equally nutritous dairy choices, as suggested on pages 84–85, and eaten during the day to boost your diet to the nutritional levels necessary for breast-feeding (see page 49 for more on this).

• I have suggested a variety of breakfasts, although if you have a special favorite or like to have roughly the same breakfast each day, by all means feel free. But do try to include a grain of some kind (for example, wheat germ, whole-grain bread, breakfast cereal). If you can include a source of vitamin C, that is helpful, too, though if you follow the rest of the day's suggestions, it's unlikely you'll be lacking in this vitamin. Equally, breakfast can be a good time to have some of your day's basic milk allowance (or equivalent in yogurt). See pages 42–46 for further information about planning your day's menus.

• Desserts are optional, but all the ones I've given are relatively simple, and some of them could be made by older children. They can be a good way of consuming extra milk.

Weaning the Baby

For the first few months of your baby's life, you won't have to worry about the baby's diet, since she will only be drinking milk, either from the breast or from the bottle.

Weaning, or getting the baby to switch from an all-milk diet to one that includes solid foods, is a process many mothers view with some apprehension. I felt that way myself; if anything it's worse for us vegetarian mothers, who may not know which vegetarian foods are suitable for a baby and may be further unsettled by anxious friends and relatives. However, the weaning process is really a very simple one, and most babies accomplish it amazingly smoothly. Parents can be reassured that a vegetarian diet can offer all the nourishment a baby needs for growth and development. This is how the weaning process might go:

WHEN THE BABY IS FOUR TO SIX MONTHS OLD

You can give the baby a little fresh, unsweetened fruit juice, diluted half-and-half with boiled, cooled water. Suitable juices are orange juice (freshly squeezed, frozen, or pasteurized, unsweetened, from a carton), or apple juice (from a carton and fortified with vitamin C, but without other additives). Apple juice is the best choice if you have any history in your family of allergies to citrus fruits. Give this fruit juice initially from a teaspoon, in the middle of the morning or afternoon. As soon as the baby gets used to taking it in this way, try giving it from a normal cup (not a mug with a feeder lid). This is an excellent way of introducing the baby to a cup. Apart from this, continue with breast- or bottle-feeding in the normal way.

Breast milk supplies all that the baby needs (including vitamin C) for the first six months of life. So if the baby is happy and thriving, there is no need to think about introducing any solids until she is six months old. If, however, after four months of age the baby does not seem fully satisfied with milk, you might try giving a first taste of food —but don't start before four months. (The danger of introducing solids early is that since the baby's immature digestive system cannot readily cope with the food, the likelihood of an allergic reaction is increased.)

The first spoonfuls are really just to get the baby used to the taste and feel of solid food. Do not think of them as a real source of nourishment at this stage. The baby still needs milk feeds for that and also for the emotional satisfaction of sucking.

The first taste of solid food should be half a teaspoonful of a fruit or vegetable puree (see pages 66–69). (Traditionally cereals were always the first solid food given to babies, but these are now advised against as they can cause allergies if given too early.)

Give this taste at one of the main milk feeds corresponding to breakfast, lunch, or dinner, whichever is the most convenient for you. (If you are planning to go back to work but want to continue to breast-feed, start giving the solids at lunchtime, for this will eventually become the first meal at which the baby gives up a breast-feeding and just has solids.)

Whether you give the first taste of solid food before or after the milk feed is up to you, or perhaps, more to the point, up to the baby! But generally speaking, it's better to give solids before the milk feed if you can so that as you gradually increase the quantity of solids, the baby will be satisfied with these and forget about the milk feed. However, there is no point in trying to give solids if the baby is hungry, wanting comfort, and crying for a feed. Better to let the baby feed first and then give the taste of solids at the end.

Be prepared for the fact that the baby may well spit out your lovingly prepared offerings. Don't worry and don't take it personally. The baby is not depending on this food for nourishment at this stage. Try again another day, persisting gently; there is no hurry.

It's a good idea to try the baby on the same food for several days before trying another, so that you can make sure there is no allergic reaction. Certainly if you have any history of allergies, asthma, hay fever, or eczema in your family, it is advisable to continue with one food for at least four days before trying another, watching the baby carefully in case there is an allergic reaction.

As the baby gets used to the flavor, you can gradually increase the quantity so that after a few weeks your baby is having perhaps two tablespoonfuls of food at a time. Increasing the quantity gradually also enables the baby's digestive system to become used to coping with solid food.

FOODS FOR WEANING AND HOW TO PREPARE THEM	
FOOD	**PREPARATION**
Carrot puree	Scrape carrot and boil it in a little unsalted water until tender; puree with enough of the cooking water to make a soft consistency. Start by giving a taste of ½ teaspoonful before or after the midday or evening milk.
Rutabaga, parsnip	Make like carrot puree.
Applesauce	Use sweet apples only, not tart ones that require added sweetening. Peel, core, and slice apple; cook in 2 to 3 tablespoons water until tender; puree, adding a little extra boiled water if necessary to make a soft consistency.
Pear puree	Make like applesauce, using sweet pears.
Banana	Choose very ripe bananas. Peel. Remove the seeds with the point of a knife if you like. Mash flesh thoroughly with a fork, adding a little cooled boiled water if necessary to make a soft consistency.

FOODS FOR WEANING AND HOW TO PREPARE THEM	
FOOD	**PREPARATION**
Avocado	Cut in half. Scoop out and mash a little of the flesh, adding a few drops of boiled water to soften if necessary.
Zucchini, lemon squash	Cut off the ends. Cut into small pieces, cook in a minimum of unsalted water until tender. Puree with enough cooking water to make a soft consistency.
Pumpkin, winter squash	Peel; remove the seeds. Cut the flesh into pieces and cook in a little boiling water until tender. Puree.
Tomato	Equally suitable either raw or cooked. Sieve cooked tomato to remove the seeds. Or scald and peel raw tomato, cut out the core, then mash. (You can remove the seeds if you like, but the jelly around them is a valuable source of soluble fiber.)
Grated apple or pear	Choose sweet apples and well-ripened pears. Peel and grate finely.
Peaches, apricots, nectarines, sweet cherries, plums, mangoes, papaya, kiwi fruit	Choose really ripe fruit. Remove the skin and pits; mash the flesh thoroughly.

FOODS FOR WEANING AND HOW TO PREPARE THEM	
FOOD	**PREPARATION**
Broccoli, cauliflower, Brussels sprouts, green cabbage	Wash and trim. Cook in a minimum of unsalted water until tender (they should be mashable but not soggy). Puree with a little of their cooking water. (Cooked cabbage and sprouts can create intestinal gas; if this is a problem, mix with another vegetable puree, such as carrot.)
Spinach	Wash thoroughly, remove the stems, shred the leaves. Cook in a saucepan without extra water until spinach is tender. Puree. (Don't give more than once or twice a week since the oxalic acid content affects the body's absorption of some minerals.)
Dried apricots, prunes, pears, peaches, apples	Wash, then cover with boiling water and soak overnight. Next day, simmer until tender. Remove pits from prunes. Puree the fruit. (Can have rather a laxative effect.)
Baby rice cereal	This is best as a first cereal because it is the least likely to cause allergic reactions. Choose one fortified with additional iron and B vitamins, and make up with liquid according to directions on the package.

FOODS FOR WEANING AND HOW TO PREPARE THEM

FOOD	PREPARATION
Potatoes	Scrub. Bake, or boil in unsalted water. Scoop potato out of skins and mash. A little very finely grated cheese, farmer cheese, cottage cheese, yogurt, tofu or milk can be added; also very finely chopped green vegetables, such as watercress or raw spinach leaves.
Corn, peas, green beans	Boil until tender; puree. Fresh or frozen are fine; canned are not advised because of the added salt and sugar.
Muesli	Buy a mix without sugar and other additives, or make your own from oats, nuts, and raisins, then grind to a powder. Moisten with water, fruit juice, or plain yogurt. Sprinkle with wheat germ, mix well. Powdered nuts or seeds or grated apple or pear can be added.
Whole-grain bread	From six months onward, a little crustless bread can be added to vegetable purees. The bran in 100% whole-grain bread and flour is too laxative for some babies; an 81–85% bread (preferably with added wheat germ, for extra iron) is often a better choice for babies under two years old.

Suggested Feeding Pattern,
from Four to Six Months

- · · · *On Waking:* Breast- or bottle-feed
- · · · *Breakfast:* Breast- or bottle-feed
- · · · *Midmorning:* Diluted real-fruit juice from spoon or cup (or give this midafternoon)
- · · · *Lunch:* ½ to 2 teaspoons fruit or vegetable puree Breast- or bottle-feed
- · · · *Midafternoon:* Diluted real-fruit juice from spoon or cup (unless this was given in the morning)
- · · · *Dinner:* Breast- or bottle-feed.
- · · · *Before bed:* Breast- or bottle-feed.

WHEN THE BABY IS
SIX TO EIGHT MONTHS OLD

You will find that as your baby takes more solid food, the demand for milk will decrease. The baby will suck from you for a shorter time and, at around eight months, may eventually give up the milk feed entirely. Your milk supply will decline correspondingly; the reverse of the process that enabled you to produce enough milk in the early days. You will probably find it takes two or three days for your body to catch up with the baby's decreased demand, and your breasts may feel rather full, but this transition period only lasts for a couple of days or so.

You can now begin to enrich the simple fruit and vegetable purees with vegetarian protein ingredients. Any of the following can be added:

VEGETARIAN PROTEIN ENRICHMENT FOODS FOR WEANING	
FOOD	**PREPARATION**
Orange lentils	Made into a thick soup, as described on page 105, these make a wonderfully nutritious meal for a baby. Serve as it is, or with a little crustless

VEGETARIAN PROTEIN ENRICHMENT FOODS FOR WEANING	
FOOD	**PREPARATION**
	whole-grain bread mashed into it; or make soup extra thick and add to a vegetable puree.
Mashed beans	Use home-cooked beans (soybeans, red kidney, cannellini, lima beans, etc.), or canned ones, well-rinsed, to remove salted water. (Don't use canned ones before baby is eight months old.) Mash thoroughly or puree.
Beans in tomato sauce	These make a quick and nutritious meal from eight months onward. Choose a variety without preservatives or colorings. (They will probably include a little salt and sugar; despite this, they're still a healthy and nutritious food.) Mash or puree. Can be mixed with crumbled whole-grain bread and a little boiled water to moisten.
Tofu	Drain tofu, mash thoroughly, then mix with vegetable or fruit purees.
Tahini, peanut butter	Mix a little—perhaps ½ teaspoonful at first—into vegetable or fruit purees. Choose (or make) a smooth peanut butter without salt or additives, such as emulsifiers and stabilizers.

VEGETARIAN PROTEIN ENRICHMENT
FOODS FOR WEANING

FOOD	PREPARATION
Yeast extract	Use a low-sodium one from the health food store. Add a little—¼ teaspoon at first—to vegetable purees.
Brewers' yeast	Use a debittered one, and sprinkle sparingly—say, ¼ teaspoonful—over baby's vegetable purees or breakfast muesli mix. Can also be added to a mashed-banana-and-yogurt mix.
Finely milled nuts and seeds	Powder the nuts in a blender, food processor or clean electric coffee grinder, or use ground almonds. If you're grinding your own, use a variety of nuts: almonds, Brazil nuts, peanuts, walnuts, pumpkin and sunflower seeds, for a full range of nutrients. Stir into fruit or vegetable purees, starting with ½ teaspoonful.
Wheat germ	Sprinkle over fruit or vegetable purees; add to cereal mixes and yogurt for splendid nourishment.
Cottage cheese, low-fat soft white cheeses such as farmer	Give this from eight months, choosing one that's preservative-free, low-salt, and, in the case of cottage cheese, not too lumpy. Mash into fruit or vegetable purees; or mix with finely shredded watercress or very finely grated carrot and a little wheat germ, brewers'

VEGETARIAN PROTEIN ENRICHMENT FOODS FOR WEANING	
FOOD	**PREPARATION**
	yeast, or yeast extract for a healthy baby salad mix!
Hard cheese	Choose a low-fat hard cheese if possible, with no colorings or preservatives. Grate finely; add to pureed vegetables, starting with ½ teaspoonful.
Yogurt	Choose an active plain yogurt without preservatives. Add to fruit purees or give as it is with a little date puree (see page 223) stirred in and a sprinkling of wheat germ and/or powdered nuts. Mashed with banana and wheat germ, and perhaps a little tahini, and some powdered nuts, this makes a quick baby meal.
Kelp powder	Add a pinch to baby's vegetable purees 3 to 4 times a week for iodine. (Available from health food stores.)
Eggs	Give just the yolk to start with; if you stir it into a hot vegetable puree, it will cook in the heat of the rest of the food. If this goes down well, try giving the yolk of a soft-boiled egg on crumbled bread. If the baby takes well to this, try lightly scrambled eggs. Don't introduce egg until the baby is eighteen to twenty-four months old if there is any history of allergies, eczema, or asthma in the family.

Once the baby is taking these solids happily, you can give an enriched vegetable puree as a main course, followed by a fruit puree or
yogurt- or cereal-based mixture as a "pudding." You can also begin
introducing solids before the other main feeds of the day, so that
eventually the feeds that correspond to breakfast, lunch, and supper
are composed entirely of solids. You will also find that as the baby gets
used to the texture of solid food, there is no need to be so particular
about pureeing the food. In fact it is good for the baby to get used
to a bit of texture in food at this stage. I soon found I only needed
to mash food for my babies, although I have heard of other babies who
were more fussy. You will gradually be able to drop first one milk feed
and then another, so that by the time the baby is around nine months
the bedtime feed may well be the only one left. Do not be in a hurry
to wean the baby from the bliss of this; it is important for the closeness
to you and the emotional satisfaction the sucking gives. Many babies
have spontaneously given up the bedtime feed by the time they are
one year old, but many have not.

Some people believe it is not a good thing to encourage feeding
during the night after, say, six months, when the baby probably
doesn't need it for nourishment but may just be acquiring an enjoy-
able habit that may drive you to distraction later on. Some recent
research at the Hospital for Sick Children, London, would seem to
confirm this view. Case studies showed that wakeful babies who were
dealt with kindly but firmly and decisively while being left in their crib
developed settled sleeping patterns within days.

Other child-care experts would disagree with this approach, and I
personally feel that if a child cries for food (and the loving comfort
of his or her mother's closeness), then it is better to meet that need,
even though this can be a demanding period. But it does pass and, I
believe, contributes very much to the child's emotional security both
at the time and, especially, in later life.

Some people suggest weaning a baby from the breast to the bottle
when you start giving solid food. I don't see any point in this unless
you want to stop breast-feeding for some reason. If the baby is happy,
you're willing to go on, and all is going well, it seems better to
continue breast-feeding for the few remaining months. However,
once the baby has given up all the daytime feeds, you might like to

give a bottle for baby's final feed so that you can be free to go out in the evenings.

At this stage, particularly if the baby is teething, you can introduce some finger foods. The baby may find it comforting to chew on something hard: a piece of apple, raw carrot, bread, or rusk, but never leave a baby alone with food like this because of the danger of choking; if anything gets stuck in the baby's throat, be ready either to hook anything out quickly with your finger or turn the baby upside down and smack *gently* in the small of the back.

Suggested Feeding Pattern, Six to Eight Months Old

- · · · *On Waking:* Breast- or bottle-feed
- · · · *Breakfast:* Baby rice or muesli cereal or enriched fruit puree
  Breast- or bottle-feed
- · · · *Midmorning:* Diluted real-fruit juice from spoon or cup (or give this midafternoon)
- · · · *Lunch:* 1 to 2 tablespoons enriched vegetable puree, or lentil puree, followed by some fruit puree for dessert (optional)
  Breast- or bottle-feed—until the baby gives this up
- · · · *Midafternoon:* Diluted real-fruit juice from spoon or cup (unless this was given in the morning)
  Finger foods: slices of apple, carrot sticks, whole wheat rusk
- · · · *Dinner:* Same as breakfast
  Breast- or bottle-feed
- · · · *Before bed:* Breast- or bottle-feed

WHEN THE BABY IS EIGHT TO TWELVE MONTHS OLD

If your baby takes well to solids, you will quite soon find that she will easily and naturally eat a little of what you, as a family, are having. If you're in doubt about the suitability of certain foods, check them against the "Cautionary Notes" on pages 81–83. The main thing to watch is that the baby's portion is not too highly seasoned or salted. Sometimes it's possible to take out a small quantity for the baby before adding spices and seasonings. If your baby gets used to trying new flavors, it will make it possible for you to eat out with friends or in a restaurant. Simply select a suitably unspiced or lightly seasoned dish from the menu—again, check the suitability of various foods—or ask for an unsalted omelet or just vegetables and grated cheese, and mash the baby's portion with a fork.

At this stage you may need to consider the amount of fiber the baby is getting. Since a vegetarian diet is naturally high in fiber, which facilitates passage of food through the intestines, it's important for the baby to have some concentrated sources of nourishment each day as well, such as egg, cheese, yogurt, powdered nuts, yeast and yeast extract (unsalted), tahini, and peanut butter. If the baby's diet becomes too laxative, it can cause a very sore bottom. It may be advisable to give a bread that is lower in fiber than whole-grain. Try wheat germ bread, or, if this is still too fibrous, get an enriched white one. Try a higher fiber bread again when the baby is a little older.

At this stage, between nine months and one year, the baby will probably have an eating plan that goes something like this:

Suggested Feeding Pattern, from Eight or Nine Months On

- · · · *On Waking:* Water or diluted real-fruit juice from cup
- · · · *Breakfast:* Muesli, Oaty Version (page 216) or oatmeal
  Whole-grain toast or bread with low-sodium yeast extract
- · · · *Midmorning:* Diluted real-fruit juice
- · · · *Lunch:* Mashed nut or legume savory with vegetables
  Fruit puree and cereal pudding, or fruit with yogurt or custard
  Water or milk
- · · · *Midafternoon:* Diluted real-fruit juice
  Finger foods: slices of apple, carrot sticks, whole wheat rusk
- · · · *Dinner:* Whole-grain bread with cottage cheese, nut butter, or lentil spread; or scrambled egg on bread or toast; or lentil soup with whole-grain bread
  Carrot sticks, pieces of raw cucumber, slices of apple
  Fruit with yogurt or cereal pudding as at lunch
  Water or milk
- · · · *Before bed:* Breast- or bottle-feed

Suggestions for Baby's Lunches

When you're preparing a midday meal for a baby or toddler, it's very convenient to be able to make something you can eat too. And it's got to be quick and easy! There are plenty of simple, delicious dishes that you can enjoy for lunch and share with your baby, either as they are or by adapting them slightly. Here are some suggestions for labor-saving shared meals:

LUNCHES BABY AND PARENT CAN SHARE		
YOUR LUNCH	**BABY'S LUNCH**	**NOTES**
Poached egg on spinach Toast or bread and butter	Pureed spinach with a little egg yolk mixed in Segments of orange, with white skin removed Milk	
Broccoli in Cheese or Almond Sauce Sliced tomato Apple	Mashed broccoli in cheese or almond sauce Finely grated apple with a little yogurt and wheat germ mixed in Milk	You can have the grated-apple dessert, too, if you prefer.

LUNCHES BABY AND PARENT CAN SHARE

YOUR LUNCH	BABY'S LUNCH	NOTES
Baked potato with grated cheese or mashed cooked beans Lettuce, tomato, and grated carrot Banana with yogurt and wheat germ	The inside of a baked potato, mashed with a little milk, grated cheese, or pureed cooked beans Banana mashed with a little yogurt and wheat germ Milk	The baby can have a little very finely grated carrot and mashed skinned tomato mixed with the potato, too.
Baked beans on whole-grain toast Watercress Sliced peach with yogurt, wheat germ, and chopped nuts	Baked beans mashed with crumbled whole-grain bread (soak in a little water if necessary to make bread mashable) Skinned peach mashed into yogurt, sprinkled with wheat germ Milk	Choose a brand of baked beans that does not have preservatives or colorings.
Quick Lentil Soup Whole-grain roll Tomato and watercress Fresh fruit	Lentil soup with whole-grain bread mashed into it Fresh fruit pieces prepared for finger-feeding Milk	Freeze leftover soup in usable portions for future use.

LUNCHES BABY AND PARENT CAN SHARE		
YOUR LUNCH	BABY'S LUNCH	NOTES
Cheese (or Tofu Spread) sandwiches Tomato, lettuce, and carrot sticks Fresh fruit	Whole-grain bread mashed in a little warm milk or soy milk with grated cheese or tofu spread Fresh fruit, mashed, grated or prepared for finger-feeding Milk	
Avocado filled with cottage cheese or tofu and shredded scallion, with lettuce, tomato, and watercress Fresh fruit	Avocado mashed with cottage cheese and very finely shredded watercress Fresh fruit, mashed, grated, or prepared for finger-feeding Milk	Choose a small, ripe avocado.
Hummus with pita bread and sprigs of raw cauliflower and carrot strips Yogurt with raisins	Hummus with whole-grain bread mashed into it Sprigs of cauliflower and carrot for finger-feeding Yogurt pureed with raisins Milk	Make or buy a hummus without much garlic. Soak the raisins in hot water or apple juice for 45 minutes or so beforehand.

LUNCHES BABY AND PARENT CAN SHARE		
YOUR LUNCH	BABY'S LUNCH	NOTES
Slice of leftover Lentil Loaf in a soft whole-grain roll, with pickle Lettuce and tomato Soaked dried apricots with yogurt	Leftover lentil loaf reheated and mashed with skinned tomato Soaked dried apricots pureed with yogurt, topped with wheat germ Milk	Buy unsulfured dried apricots and soak overnight.
Cottage cheese or fermented nut cheese Salad of lettuce, tomato, grated raw beet, and grated carrot Whole-grain toast or roll	Cottage cheese or fermented nut cheese mashed with skinned tomato, finely grated beet, and carrot Fingers of whole-grain bread or toast and yeast extract Milk	Choose a low-salt or unsalted cottage cheese.
Red Kidney Bean Salad on lettuce with alfalfa sprouts, tomato, and grated carrot Whole-grain bread Apple, raw, or baked with filling of dates and wheat germ, topped with yogurt	Red kidney beans mashed with finely chopped lettuce, alfalfa, and finely grated carrot Fingers of whole-grain bread or toast and yeast extract Finger-food slices of raw apple, or finely grated apple, or mashed	Canned beans (without coloring) are fine from age eight months on. Put beans into a sieve and rinse under cold water to remove some of the brine.

LUNCHES BABY AND PARENT CAN SHARE		
YOUR LUNCH	**BABY'S LUNCH**	**NOTES**
	baked apple and date with yogurt Milk	
Scrambled egg or tofu on whole-grain toast Watercress Orange	Scrambled egg or tofu on crumbled whole-grain bread Skinned orange segments for finger eating Milk	

CAUTIONARY NOTES ON FOODS FOR YOUNG BABIES	
FOOD	**REASON**
Salt, and salty foods, including chips, savory snacks, salted stock, soy sauce, and yeast extracts (except low sodium)	Too much salt is not good for anyone; in babies under eighteen months it can put excessive strain on (and even possibly damage) the liver and kidneys.
Spices, including curry powder, pepper, nutmeg, and mustard	Same as above.
Refined flour and flour products	Often contain additives, such as bleaching agents, preservatives, and so on, and may also contain traces of chemicals used in the growing process (fertilizer, pesticides), which can cause allergies. But 100% whole-grain flour and bread may be too high in fiber for some babies under twelve months (see page 69).

CAUTIONARY NOTES ON FOODS FOR YOUNG BABIES	
FOOD	**REASON**
Sugar, and food and drink containing this, such as syrups and jams (Raw, turbinado sugar can be used sparingly from two years on.)	Contains no nutrients, only calories. Because it lacks fiber, it is taken into the bloodstream too quickly, causing the body to produce large amounts of insulin. Over a prolonged period, this has been linked with the development of mature-onset diabetes. Raw, turbinado sugar does contain some nutrients, such as iron, calcium, and B vitamins, but this, too, should be restricted because of the lack of fiber. Dried and fresh fruit, date puree, honey, natural fruit juices, and no-added-sugar jams are a better source of sweetness in the diet.
Honey (Small amounts of real organic honey can be used from twelve months on.)	Another concentrated food, which is why it is not recommended for young babies. It does not contain fiber, so it has the same disadvantages as sugar, except that honey contains natural antibiotics and has been found to have healing properties.
Processed, canned and packaged foods containing additives such as preservatives, emulsifiers, artificial flavorings and colorings	Not recommended at any age, but especially not for babies because of the danger of allergic reactions. Some additives have been linked with hyperactivity and aggression in young children. Permissible ones, in my

CAUTIONARY NOTES ON FOODS FOR YOUNG BABIES	
FOOD	**REASON**
	opinion, include canned beans, baked beans, and tomatoes.
Whole nuts, both salted and unsalted (Unsalted whole nuts can be given from about five or six years on.)	They can get stuck in the baby's throat and cause choking. Salted nuts have the additional disadvantages described under Salt.
Caffeine (found in coffee, tea, cola drinks, chocolate, and products made from cocoa)	It is a stimulant.
Alcohol	Because of its undesirable effects and also because in countries where it is normal to give young children diluted wine, this is being linked with alcoholism later in life.
Deep-fried foods	Fat is difficult for a baby to digest, and too much fat is undesirable in any diet. Heating oil to the temperatures required for deep frying alters the chemical structure, making it potentially harmful (see page 14).

Feeding the Vegetarian Toddler

While babies will usually eat what they're given, often with great relish, when they get to the toddler stage (between ages fifteen months and four years) and develop minds of their own, feeding can become more of a problem. They often have passionate likes and dislikes, and I've met many mothers who are worried that their toddler hardly seems to be eating enough to keep a sparrow alive. I've been through this stage with my own children, so I know the kind of inner panic that can set in as yet another meal is barely touched. Pediatricians say reassuringly that no child of this age will starve in the face of food, so if your child is obviously thriving, in spite of minuscule meals, then you do not have to worry too much. The most important thing is for you to remain calm and not allow a tense atmosphere to build up at mealtimes.

It is important with children of this age, even if their tastes are faddish, to make sure that everything they do eat is as nourishing as possible. One problem with a vegetarian/vegan diet is that many of the foods, although nutritious, are also rather high in fiber, and while that is a good thing for adults, the amount of chewing involved may mean that young children do not eat enough to obtain all the nutrients they need. So it's best to choose foods that provide nutrients in a concentrated form.

If you can possibly do so, try to get your child to drink 2½ cups milk or soy milk (fortified with calcium and riboflavin) each day. This will ensure that his requirements for riboflavin and calcium are pretty well covered, as well as providing half or more of the day's protein, valuable zinc, vitamin A, and, in the case of soy milk, almost a quarter of the day's iron requirement. Milk can of course be consumed in many other ways than as a plain drink; it can be eaten in the form of yogurt, flavored and lightly sweetened if necessary; on breakfast cereals; as frozen pops, frothy milk shakes, ice cream, puddings; in the form of cottage cheese (perhaps as a snack in celery sticks or as a dip with carrot strips) or cheese (perhaps in sandwiches or in cubes, with apple). Milk will also supply over a quarter of the day's thiamine requirement.

A young child's need for thiamine (see page 16) can be met almost entirely by a 1-ounce serving of a fortified whole wheat breakfast cereal. Other sources of thiamine are whole-grain bread, legumes, Brazil nuts, dried fruit, and yeast extract, some or all of which will probably be eaten during the course of the day, so a standard vegetarian/vegan toddler diet presents no problem here. One alternative to the fortified breakfast cereal could be a mixture of ¼ cup finely grated Brazil nuts, 3 chopped or pureed dates, and ½ tablespoon (or more) wheat germ; this provides nearly six-sevenths of the daily thiamine needs and can be added to a few rolled oats for a muesli mix or to plain yogurt. Or, for older children, the dates can be stuffed with the Brazil nuts and the wheat germ can be added to something else during the day, or sprinkled over whatever breakfast cereal is the current favorite.

Niacin requirements (see page 19) are a little more difficult to meet, so this is a nutrient that needs watching. Fortified breakfast cereals are a good source, and a 1-ounce serving of breakfast cereal, plus the milk and 2 slices of bread already suggested, will supply around 5.5 mg.

Iron is another nutrient you need to keep your eye on. However, if your toddler has 2 slices of whole-grain bread a day, supplying 1.0 mg, plus an iron-enriched cereal, these together will supply around a fifth of his daily requirements. If your child is consuming 2 cups of soy milk, that will supply another 3.6 mg.

Vitamin C is unlikely to be a problem. The whole of the recommended daily allowance (see page 25) can be supplied by 3 to 4 ounces of orange or grapefruit, 2 tangerines, ⅓ cup orange juice, or one large tomato, or by ½ cup of strawberries!

These are also all sources of Vitamin A as well (see page 26). And the recommended amount of milk supplies half, as does ½ pat of butter or margarine. Carrots are also an excellent source of this vitamin, and just ½ ounce of raw carrots will supply the entire day's allowance of vitamin A.

Vitamin D can be more of a problem. Vegetarians eating dairy products can get nearly one-quarter of their RDA (see page 28) from 1 ounce of fortified margarine, and breakfast cereals fortified with vitamin D can also supply some, as can cheese, milk, eggs, and yogurt. For most children, however, a vitamin D supplement, in the form of drops, is a sensible precaution.

Many people worry about getting enough protein in a vegetarian diet. But as I explained on page 6, a vegetarian diet that contains adequate amounts of calcium, iron, and B vitamins will automatically contain enough protein.

PUTTING IT INTO PRACTICE

To sum up, the following foods provide an excellent nutritional basis for the toddler's day:

- · · · 2½ cups milk or soy milk or equivalent in cheese or yogurt
- · · · 1 ounce vitamin-enriched breakfast cereal, or the equivalent described
- · · · 2 good slices whole-grain bread
- · · · ⅓ cup orange juice or 3 to 4 ounces orange
- · · · Vitamin D and, if necessary, B_{12} supplement
- · · · Pinch of kelp or use of iodized salt or seaweed jelling agents
  To this you need to add, in particular, foods that are rich in iron. Children of this age can be extremely fussy, and some foods will be more readily accepted than others, so choose wisely. Some suggestions would be 1 to 2 daily servings of legumes, peanut butter, almonds, or pumpkin seeds; a serving of potato or grain such as brown rice, millet, whole wheat pasta or whole-grain bread (in addition to the above); dried fruit (including prune juice if liked); yeast extract; wheat germ; and as many raw and cooked vegetables (including a daily serving of leafy vegetables if possible) as your child will eat.

Here's how this scheme works out in terms of meals:

Menu Plans for the Vegetarian/Vegan Toddler

- · · · *Breakfast*
  Fortified whole-grain cereal with milk or soy milk, a sprinkling of wheat germ, raisins; whole-grain toast with yeast extract; milk

OR rolled oats, flaked millet, and wheat germ soaked in prune juice with chopped dates and grated Brazil nuts; milk

OR chopped banana, wheat germ, grated Brazil nuts, chopped dates, yogurt; whole-grain toast with yeast extract; milk

OR cereal or oat mix as above; soft-boiled egg with fingers of whole-grain bread or toast; milk

· · · *Midmorning and/or Afternoon*

Orange juice diluted with a little water (or prune juice, if your toddler is getting enough vitamin C from other sources, see page 25)

· · · *Lunch and Dinner (see below)*

· · · *Bedtime*

Milk

In planning the menus below, I have allowed a legume dish either at lunch or dinner; a green vegetable either at lunch or dinner; bread/cereal at either or both; a fruit and milk pudding or its equivalent. Make sure that your toddler is getting 2½ cups (20 fl oz) milk or calcium-fortified soy milk during the day.

ONE WEEK'S MENUS FOR TODDLER'S LUNCH AND DINNER	
LUNCH	**DINNER**
Pureed spinach with a little egg yolk mixed in Toast or bread with butter or margarine Segments of orange Milk	Whole-grain bread with Lentil Spread and slices of tomato Grated apple with yogurt, raisins, and wheat germ Milk
Mashed Broccoli in Cheese or Almond Sauce Sliced tomato Finely grated apple with a little yogurt and wheat germ Milk	Hummus with fingers of whole-grain toast Carrot sticks Millet and Raisin Cream Milk

ONE WEEK'S MENUS FOR TODDLER'S LUNCH AND DINNER

LUNCH	DINNER
Baked potato mashed with a little finely grated cheese or tofu and finely grated carrot Banana mashed with a little yogurt and grated pumpkin seeds Milk	Lentil soup and whole-grain roll Raw broccoli florets Ripe pear slices Milk
Lentil soup with whole-grain bread mashed into it Tomato pieces Fresh fruit pieces prepared for finger-feeding Milk	Mushroom Soup with milk (see page 106) Watercress sandwiches Carob Pudding Milk
Whole-grain bread mashed in a little warm milk or soy milk with grated cheese or mashed legumes Carrot sticks Pieces of apple, grated or prepared for finger-feeding Milk	Baked beans on toast Apples with Raisins, pureed, with yogurt and wheat germ Milk
Leftover Lentil Loaf, reheated and mashed with skinned tomato Soaked dried apricots pureed with yogurt, topped with sprinkling of wheat germ Milk	Potato Cakes with Nuts Carrot sticks Muesli: yogurt mixed with rolled oats, wheat germ, finely grated apple, raisins, powdered pumpkin seeds Milk
Scrambled egg or tofu on crumbled whole-grain bread Shredded watercress Segments of orange Milk	Red Kidney Bean Salad with lettuce, sprouted legumes, and carrot sticks Fingers of whole-grain bread with yeast extract Slices of raw apple Milk

EATING BETWEEN MEALS: HEALTHY SNACKS

Snacks between meals are not necessarily a bad thing if they're nutritious. They may be the most acceptable and harmonious way of getting nourishment into a difficult toddler! Here are some ideas for between-meal nibbles that contribute positively to the diet:

- · · · Carrot sticks
- · · · Celery sticks filled with low-fat ricotta, tofu spread, or peanut butter
- · · · Fingers of whole-grain toast (or whole-grain rusks) with peanut butter
- · · · Figs, dates, raisins, and dried apricots
- · · · Whole almonds, Brazil nuts, and pumpkin seeds (given under supervision in case of choking, from around five years old)
- · · · Homemade nut and fruit sweets (see pages 231–33)
- · · · Yogurt-and-fruit milk shakes
- · · · Homemade yogurt or orange juice ice pops
- · · · Nutty carob bananas
- · · · Healthy ice cream
- · · · Cubes of cheese

SURVIVAL TIPS

• Do not worry if your child really does not like some food; you can usually find another source of the same nutrients. It's better to stick to foods you know will go down well—and avoid battles of will.

• All children go through the stage when they learn the power of the word no. If this veto is used over food, you may be able to nip it in the bud by offering a choice of two equally nutritious items instead of single suggestions they can veto.

• Encourage your toddler to feed herself from an early age. Yes, it's horribly messy, but a sensible bib—the plastic ones with pockets in which to catch spilled food are good—and some kind of easily washed or disposable covering on the floor under the baby's chair, such as newspaper, will cope with most disasters.

• Do not worry if your toddler eats the foods in the "wrong" order or mixes things up (after all, that's part of the fun, spoilsport!); and don't set too high a standard. The toddler will enjoy being independent, and competence will grow with practice. You'll bless it in the end!

• If there's a problem over food, the secret is not to get emotional about it either because you're worried about your toddler's health or because it's hurtful to have your food refused. It simply isn't worth making an issue over food or allowing a difficult situation to develop. In fact, as in all things concerning your child, it's your relationship with him or her that's the most important thing. This is what you're building up and what will endure long after you've forgotten the horrors of broken nights, tantrums, food fads, and puddles on the carpet! Always put this relationship first, before a spotless house, before rigid timetables, before battles over food or anything else, and you will be rewarded by the deepening bond of understanding and companionship that will develop between you.

PART

2

The Recipes

Introduction

In order to qualify for inclusion in this book, recipes had to be nutritious, health-giving, and easy to make; the ones in the quick recipe section had to be particularly easy. While I was working on this section I had vivid memories of the many times I've prepared a meal with one hand while comforting a crying baby by holding her over my shoulder with the other. In addition to the very quick recipes, I've included a section of ones that freeze well so that you can stock up the freezer before the baby arrives. You'll also find recipes for nutritious salads and soups, with suggestions for making both into main courses; nourishing drinks you can whizz up to sustain you when you're breast-feeding; sandwiches, dips, and spreads; easy, wholesome cakes and sweets; and a few special baby foods for weaning.

Drinks

Drinks can be an excellent source of nourishment when you're pregnant and not feeling much like cooking or eating, or when you're breast-feeding and need to keep up your energy with the minimum of fuss. You will find these drinks most beneficial if you can sip them slowly while you relax or feed the baby.

In addition to the drinks given here, it's a good idea to keep a large jug of water in the refrigerator. You will need to drink water to replace lost fluid when you're breast-feeding, and many people find tap water more pleasant when it's really cold. Even better would be tap water that has been passed through a water filter.

APRICOT, ORANGE, AND ALMOND WHIZZ

This drink, and the one that follows, is particularly good after a Caesarean section or when you've had a number of stitches, because it contains vitamins A and C, which help the wounds to heal, plus iron to help replenish supplies depleted through bleeding. The apricots do need soaking beforehand (this applies even to those that say they're ready to use, so I don't see any advantage in paying more for these). If you like this recipe, though, it might be worth soaking a larger quantity and keeping the remainder in the refrigerator, ready for when you need them.

Makes 1½ cups

>*2 ounces dried apricots, unsulfured if possible*
>*1¼ cups orange juice*
>*1 to 2 teaspoons honey*
>*1 ounce almonds, blanched*
>*1 tablespoon wheat germ*

Wash the apricots carefully in warm water. Put them into a bowl, cover with boiling water, and leave to soak for a few hours, or overnight if possible. Then drain the apricots and put them into a blender with the orange juice, honey, almonds, and wheat germ. Whizz for about 1 minute, or until smooth. Pour into a tall glass.

APRICOT AND ORANGE NECTAR

A lighter drink that, like the previous one, supplies vitamins A and C, as well as some iron and calcium, to help heal tissues after the birth.

Makes 1 glass

> *2 ounces dried apricots, unsulfured if possible*
> *1 cup orange juice*
> *1 to 2 teaspoons honey*
> *1 teaspoon brewers' yeast*

Wash and soak the apricots as in the previous recipe, then put into a blender with the orange juice, honey, and yeast and whizz to a puree. Pour into a glass and serve. In hot weather this is good with some ice cubes added.

BANANA MILK SHAKE

This drink, adapted from the one Barbara Griggs gives in *The Home Herbal,* is a palatable way to take nutritious brewers' yeast and is rich in iron and calcium.

Makes 1 glass

> *1 banana, peeled*
> *1 cup milk or soy milk*

2 heaping tablespoons plain yogurt or Vegan Yogurt (page 219)
2 teaspoons brewers' yeast

Cut the banana into rough chunks. Place it in a blender with the rest of the ingredients. Whizz until smooth and frothy; serve at once.

CAROB SHAKE

The carob gives this a deliciously rich chocolaty flavor as well as providing iron and calcium. This is another particularly good drink to have when you're feeling drained and in need of a quick boost of energy and is a good way of taking milk or soy milk if you don't like drinking them in their natural state.

Makes 1 glass

> *1½ teaspoons carob powder*
> *1 teaspoon honey*
> *1 tablespoon skim-milk powder or soy flour*
> *1 cup milk or soy milk*
> *Pinch of cinnamon*

Put the carob, honey, and skim-milk powder or soy flour into a small bowl and blend to a smooth paste with a little of the milk or soy milk. Heat the rest of the milk to boiling, then pour it onto the carob mixture, stirring well. Pour back into the pan and heat for a moment or two, to make it piping hot, then serve as it is, garnished with cinnamon, or pour into a blender and whizz for a few seconds if you want a foamy top.

FORTIFIED MILK

This is another way of making milk palatable if you don't like drinking it plain. The addition of skim-milk powder gives the milk a lovely rich taste, without adding many calories, as well as increasing the calcium. This one glass of fortified milk has double the calcium of an ordinary glass of milk. Other ingredients can be added according to taste: a little honey and/or a pinch of cinnamon, for instance.

Makes 1 glass

> 1 cup milk
> 2 heaping tablespoons skim-milk powder

Simply put the ingredients into a blender and whizz together. You can heat the milk first if you prefer a hot drink.

LASSI

This drink from India is refreshing in hot weather and is also nourishing because of the protein and calcium in the yogurt. It can be made either salty or sweet, according to taste. If you want to increase your milk supply, try adding a teaspoonful of the seeds of fennel, dill, cumin, caraway, or anise to this mixture. These are traditional herbal remedies for shortage of milk in breast-feeding and also act as a general tonic and antidepressant.

Makes 1 glass

> 1 big tablespoon plain yogurt or Vegan Yogurt (page 219)
> 7 ounces water, chilled
> Pinch of salt, or 1 to 2 teaspoons honey and pinch of cinnamon,
>   or a few drops of triple-strength rose water, or 1 teaspoon
>   fennel, dill, cumin, caraway, or anise seeds, steeped in a
>   tablespoon of boiling water and cooled

Put the yogurt into a glass and gradually stir in the water. Add the salt or honey and cinnamon or rose water or the water in which the seeds were soaked (you can add the seeds, too, if you like, but this isn't essential).

MISO PICK-ME-UP

A hot, savory drink containing B vitamins.

Makes 1 glass

> *1¼ cups hot water*
> *1 to 2 teaspoons miso*
> *2 to 3 tablespoons chopped watercress*
> *Sea salt to taste if necessary (miso is already quite salty)*

Put the hot water into a glass and stir in the miso, watercress, and salt if desired.

YOGURT-AND-ORANGE FLIP

This is a favorite drink of mine, pregnant or not. It's rich in vitamins A, B, and C and also contains calcium. It's particularly good after a Caesarean or if you've had to have stitches, because the vitamins help the healing process, and it's also calming and revitalizing.

Makes approximately 1 glass

> *1 orange, peeled*
> *5 ounces plain yogurt or Vegan Yogurt (see page 219)*
> *Honey (optional)*

Break the orange into segments and place in a blender. Add the yogurt, and whizz for 30 to 60 seconds, until fairly smooth. Add a little honey to taste if you like. There will still be some chunky pieces of orange, but these give the drink a pleasant "body" and provide extra fiber.

HERB TEAS

Herb teas can be very pleasant and beneficial. The herb tea bags you can get from health food stores are convenient to use and come in a wide range of varieties. They contain enough herbs to make a pleasant drink rather than a herbal medicine; for a stronger effect, use two teabags to a cupful of boiling water. Or you can make your own herb tea from dried or fresh herbs. Herb teas that are particularly useful for pregnancy and childbirth are peppermint, for digestive problems; and chamomile, which is soothing, sleep-inducing, and can be given cooled, to a restless baby as well. Peppermint, chamomile, or linden tea, taken first thing in the morning, can be helpful for morning sickness. Raspberry leaf tea is a traditional and well-tried herbal treatment for pregnancy and can be safely taken, unless you've been doing a great deal of physical exercise and have very well developed stomach muscles, in which case its muscle-toning effect might be too much. Drink a cupful of raspberry leaf tea three times a day during pregnancy and during the postnatal period.

Soups

Soups are easy to make. If you doubt this, try the Quick Lentil Soup, the preparation for which takes about 10 minutes; or the Lima Bean and Tomato Soup, or the Thick Leek and Potato Soup, which are also very quick to do.

When you're pregnant, especially in the early days, soup may be just what you fancy, and homemade soup can be a good source of nourishment. You can make it more filling—turn it into a main course, in fact—by serving it with whole wheat bread or rolls or with hot whole wheat garlic bread. To make this, you need a loaf of whole wheat Italian bread. Slice the loaf without going right through the bottom crust, so that all the slices hold together. Cream 1 or 2 large crushed garlic cloves into ¼ pound (1 stick) butter, then spread the slices of bread on both sides with this. Press the loaf together, wrap in foil, and bake at 400°F for about 20 minutes, or until the butter has melted and the crust of the bread is crisp. Serve immediately.

Sesame toast is also good with soup. To make this, toast whole wheat bread on one side. Butter the untoasted side, sprinkle generously with sesame seeds, and toast under the broiler until golden brown and crisp.

QUICK SEAWEED STOCK

Please don't be deterred from making soup because you have no stock at hand; perfectly good soup can be made using plain water with or without a vegetarian stock cube or powder. If you've saved the cooking water from vegetables (which I hope you have, because of the B vitamins and minerals it contains), use this as stock. If you have time, enrich it even further by rinsing a small handful of dulse (a type of seaweed you can buy from health food stores), adding this to the vegetable water, and letting it soak for several hours, or simmering it in the water for 15 to 20 minutes. Strain and discard the seaweed before using the stock.

EASY BORSCHT

This is quick to make, because it calls for canned beets. To make it into a main course, serve with grated cheese or a savory seed mix (see pages 186–87), plus garlic bread, cooked brown rice, or a baked potato. It's also nice topped with a spoonful of plain yogurt or, for a touch of luxury, sour cream. Borscht can be sprinkled with some caraway or dill seeds if you like, and these are a natural remedy for increasing the milk supply.

Serves 4

> 2 large onions, peeled and chopped
> 2 tablespoons oil
> 2 cups cabbage (spring or savoy), washed and shredded
> 1 pound canned beets, with liquid (4 cups altogether)
> Two 16-ounce cans tomatoes, with liquid
> 3 cups water
> 1 tablespoon tomato puree
> 1 tablespoon wine or apple cider vinegar
> Sea salt
> Freshly ground black pepper
> A little sugar to taste

Fry the onions gently in the oil for 7 minutes, or until soft but not brown. Then add the cabbage and cook for 3 minutes more, stirring often. Meanwhile, dice the beets. Add to the onions, along with the tomatoes, water, tomato puree, and vinegar. Cook gently for 15 minutes. Season to taste with salt, pepper, and sugar.

TO FREEZE. Cook completely, let cool, and freeze for up to 2 months. To use, allow to defrost for several hours, then heat gently, stirring.

LIMA BEAN AND TOMATO SOUP

This is quick to make, using either your own frozen lima beans (see page 54) or a canned version. It's nutritious enough to serve as a main course and even more so if you add a dollop of plain yogurt, a spoonful of savory seed mix (see pages 186–87), or some grated cheese for extra calcium. Good with whole wheat rolls, garlic bread, or a baked potato. Like borscht, this soup is also nice topped with sour cream when the budget allows.

Serves 4

> 2 large onions, peeled and chopped
> 2 tablespoons oil
> 2 cups home-cooked lima beans plus 1 cup cooking liquid (see
>   page 101) or two 16-ounce cans, with liquid
> Two 15-ounce cans tomatoes, with liquid
> 2 tablespoons tomato puree
> Sea salt
> Freshly ground black pepper
> A little sugar to taste, if necessary

Fry the onions gently in the oil for 10 minutes, or until soft but not brown. Drain the beans, keeping the liquid. Add the beans and tomatoes to the onions. Add enough water to the reserved liquid to make 2½ cups and add to the pan, together with the tomato puree. Cook gently for about 5 minutes, or until everything is heated through. Season to taste with salt, pepper, and sugar.

TO FREEZE. Cook completely, let cool, and freeze for up to 2 months. To use, allow to defrost for several hours, then heat gently, stirring. Do not freeze if you have used frozen beans to make the soup, since the texture will not be good.

THICK LEEK AND POTATO SOUP

Warming and soothing, this soup can be served with grated cheese or the savory seed mix on pages 186–87. Or it can be eaten as is, sprinkled with lots of chopped parsley, with a protein course such as crackers and cheese or with a protein such as yogurt, muesli pudding, or a handful of nuts and raisins to follow.

Serves 4

> *2 tablespoons butter*
> *1 tablespoon oil*
> *1 large onion, peeled and chopped*
> *2 pounds potatoes, peeled and cut into chunks*
> *1½ pounds leeks, washed, trimmed, and sliced*
> *2 cups water*
> *1 cube vegetable bouillon*
> *Sea salt*
> *Freshly ground black pepper*
> *Chopped parsley (optional)*

Heat the butter and oil in a large saucepan. When the butter has melted, put in the onion and fry gently for 5 minutes. Then add the potatoes and leeks and fry gently for 5 minutes more, stirring often. Pour in the water, crumble in the bouillon cube, stir, and bring to a boil. Then cover and leave to cook gently for about 15 minutes, or until the vegetables are just tender. Check the seasoning, then serve, sprinkled with chopped parsley if you have it.

QUICK LENTIL SOUP

Very soothing and nourishing and another excellent source of iron.
This soup is very popular with the babies of my acquaintance and was
the first food I gave my youngest daughter, when she was six months
old. Serve with warm whole wheat rolls or garlic bread.

Serves 4

> 1 onion, peeled and chopped
> 2 tablespoons butter or margarine
> 1 clove garlic, peeled and minced
> ½ pound split red lentils
> 4 cups water
> 1 to 2 tablespoons lemon juice
> Sea salt
> Freshly ground black pepper
> Chopped parsley (optional)

Fry the onion gently in the butter or margarine for 10 minutes, or
until soft. Add the garlic, lentils, and water. Bring to a boil, then
simmer gently for 15 to 20 minutes, or until the lentils are soft and
pale-colored. You can either beat the soup with a spoon, to break up
the lentils, or let cool a bit and puree it in a blender, for a smooth,
creamy texture. Add the lemon juice and salt and pepper to taste.
Return to the pan and reheat before serving. It's delicious with some
chopped parsley sprinkled over the top.

MUSHROOM SOUP

Mushrooms are an excellent source of niacin, so this is a useful and nourishing soup for vegetarians and vegans.

Serves 4

> 1 onion, peeled and chopped
> 1 tablespoon butter or margarine
> 1 clove garlic, peeled and crushed
> ½ pound button mushrooms, washed and sliced
> ½ pound potatoes, peeled and cubed
> 1½ cups water
> 1½ cups milk or soy milk
> 1 to 2 tablespoons lemon juice
> Dash of yeast extract
> Sea salt
> Freshly ground black pepper
> Chopped parsley (optional)
> Light cream or soy milk (optional)

Fry the onion gently in the butter or margarine for 5 minutes. Add the garlic, mushrooms, and potatoes and fry over a very gentle heat, covered, for 10 to 15 minutes more. Add the water and milk, bring to a boil, then simmer gently for 15 to 20 minutes, or until the potatoes are soft. Let cool a bit, puree in a blender, then return the soup to the pan and add the lemon juice, yeast extract, and salt and pepper to taste. Sprinkle with chopped parsley before serving. A little light cream or soy milk is nice swirled on top, too, for a treat.

TOMATO AND FRESH BASIL SOUP WITH CREAM

When made from fresh tomatoes and basil from the garden, this has to be one of the best soups of all. If you don't have any basil, use chopped tarragon or chives instead. This is another soup I like chilled in the summer.

Serves 4 to 6

> 2 tablespoons butter or margarine—or 2 tablespoons oil if
>   you're going to serve it chilled
> 1 onion, peeled and chopped
> ¾ pound potatoes, peeled and cut into even-size chunks
> 1 pound tomatoes, peeled and chopped
> 4½ cups light vegetable stock or water
> Sea salt
> Freshly ground black pepper
> ½ teaspoon sugar
> ⅔ cup light cream
> 2 tablespoons chopped fresh basil

Melt the butter or margarine, or heat the oil, in a large saucepan and add the onion. Sauté for 5 to 7 minutes, or until fairly soft but not brown. Add the potatoes and cook for 2 to 3 minutes more, stirring often. Add the tomatoes, mix, then pour in the stock or water and bring to a boil. Turn the heat down, cover, and simmer for about 20 minutes, or until the potatoes are soft. Puree the soup, then pour it through a strainer into a clean saucepan to move the seeds of the tomatoes. Season with salt, pepper, and sugar. Reheat and serve each bowlful topped with a swirl of cream and sprinkling of basil.

WATERCRESS SOUP

Watercress is rich in iron and calcium and, when cooked (so that you eat enough of it), it can be a good source of these nutrients. This soup, therefore, is a soothing and delicious way of taking a dose of minerals. I find it to be a marvelous tonic when I'm feeling tired.

Serves 4

> *1 pound potatoes, peeled and cut into even-size pieces*
> *3½ cups water*
> *2 cubes vegetable bouillon*
> *2 large bunches watercress*
> *1 tablespoon potato flour or cornmeal*
> *5 ounces light cream or milk*
> *½ to 1 teaspoon miso (optional)*
> *Sea salt*
> *Freshly ground black pepper*
> *Grated nutmeg*

Put the potatoes, water, and stock cubes into a large saucepan. Wash and chop the watercress. Reserve 2 tablespoons. Add the rest to the saucepan, together with the stems. Bring to a boil, then simmer gently for about 15 minutes, or until the potatoes are tender. Let cool a bit, then puree in a blender. Mix the potato flour or cornmeal with the cream or milk and add this to the soup, stirring. Simmer the soup for 5 to 10 minutes more. Add the reserved watercress leaves and the miso if you're using it. Season to taste with salt, pepper, and nutmeg.

Salads

There is no magic about cooking that makes hot food more nutritious. A salad you've quickly put together can be just as nutritious as—often more so than—a "good cooked meal." So if you don't feel like cooking when you're pregnant, or if salads are more convenient for you to organize when you're busy with the baby, don't feel you are depriving yourself or your family of any vital nutrients.

Salads can be made from most raw vegetables except potatoes, eggplant, and Jerusalem artichokes, and a salad made from vegetables that are in season can be very economical. For speed, I generally mix a quick oil and vinegar dressing straight into the salad bowl, then put in all the salad ingredients and mix gently. Although olive oil has as superb flavor, for the sake of nourishment I suggest a cold-pressed corn oil or safflower oil, or a small quantity of wheat germ oil mixed with olive oil. This will ensure that your vitamin E needs are covered.

SALAD DRESSINGS

YOGURT DRESSING

Plenty of parsley added to this increases its calcium and iron content and gives a pretty color. I also like this dressing very much served with hot nut and legume savories.

Makes about 1¼ cups

> 1¼ cups plain yogurt
> 1 to 2 heaping tablespoons finely chopped fresh herbs, especially
>   parsley, chives, and mint
> 1 tablespoon lemon juice
> Sea salt
> Freshly ground black pepper

Put the yogurt into a bowl and stir in the chopped herbs, lemon juice, and salt and pepper to taste.

IF YOU DON'T EAT DAIRY PRODUCTS. Use Vegan Yogurt (page 219).

VARIATIONS
Add some grated cucumber, too, or leave out the herbs and use 2 tablespoons finely chopped red or green pepper, or some coarsely grated carrot and a few raisins.

TOFU DRESSING

This is a bit like mayonnaise but considerably more nutritious, since it contains useful amounts of iron and calcium, among other things. If you're not sure what tofu is, see page 57.

Makes about 1 cup

> 10½ ounces soft tofu
> 2 teaspoons wine vinegar
> 1 teaspoon dry mustard
> 1 teaspoon turbinado or brown sugar
> 2 tablespoons oil
> Sea salt
> Freshly ground black pepper

If you've got a blender or food processor, simply put all the ingredients into the container and whizz together until combined. Alternatively, put the tofu into a bowl and whisk until smooth, then add the vinegar, mustard, and sugar and whisk again. Then beat in the oil, a little at a time. Season to taste with salt and pepper. This is also nice with some chopped fresh herbs or scallions added.

VINAIGRETTE DRESSING

The secret of a good vinaigrette lies almost entirely in the quality of the ingredients. If you use a really fine olive oil, a good red wine vinegar, sea salt, and freshly ground black pepper—and remember the proportions three or four parts oil to one of vinegar—you really can't fail!

Serves 4 to 6

> *1 tablespoon wine vinegar*
> *3 or 4 tablespoons oil*
> *Sea salt*
> *Freshly ground black pepper*

Mix together the vinegar and 3 tablespoons of oil. Add a good seasoning of salt and pepper—remember the dressing will be weakened by being served with other ingredients so it needs to be well seasoned. Taste the dressing and, if it's too vinegary, add the remaining oil until you get the flavor just right. Pour the dressing into a small jug or bowl and blend it again before you serve it. A small wire whisk is particularly handy to ensure the complete blending of oil and vinegar, which separate so easily. This dressing is also nice with a tablespoon of chopped herbs added, or a little mustard, depending on what you're going to serve it with; a generous dollop of brown mustard (whisked in) will make the consistency creamy and smooth. It's fun to experiment once you've got the basic mixture right.

HOW TO SPROUT BEANS AND SEEDS

Sprouted beans and seeds are highly nutritious and full of the life force of the emerging shoot. I like them at any time, but they seem particularly appropriate to eat when you're pregnant, especially if you find ordinary cooked beans a little heavy or indigestible. You can sprout most legumes; my favorites are chick-peas, the little green mung beans, and green lentils. Soybeans make excellent sprouts, and I find this the most palatable way of eating these nutritious legumes. Alfalfa and triticale, a kind of wheat, which you can get at health food stores, are also excellent.

To sprout beans or seeds, put four heaping tablespoons of your chosen type into a large jar, cover with water, and allow to stand overnight. Next day cover the top of the jar with a piece of cheese cloth or muslin secured with an elastic band. Drain the beans or seeds by pouring out the water through the cloth. Then, right through the cloth, fill the jar with cold water, swish it around, and drain it out again. Leave the jar on its side by the sink so that additional water can drain. Repeat the rinsing process twice a day. The sprouts will take 2 to 5 days; they are ready to eat when the shoot is the same length as the bean or seed, except for alfalfa, in which the shoots can get longer, up to about 1 inch. You can also buy a special sprouter, which consists of three tiers of shallow trays with holes in the base. This enables you to have three different types of legume sprouting at once, or one type in three different stages, so that you have a nonstop supply. The sprouts are easily watered through the top and then drip into a tray at the base, which collects the water. I find this device to be a boon, and it keeps my kitchen tidy. When the sprouts are ready, they can be kept in the refrigerator for several days. Use the whole thing, shoot and seed, for a lovely crunchy salad or stir fry. The only legumes it is inadvisable to sprout are red kidney beans, which contain a substance that can cause stomach upsets unless the beans are boiled for at least 10 minutes before eating.

ALFALFA SLAW

Serves 4

> *3 cups grated cabbage*
> *2 carrots, grated*
> *1 cup alfalfa sprouts*
> *Vinaigrette Dressing (page 111)*

Mix together all the vegetables; add enough Vinaigrette Dressing to moisten.

AVOCADO AND MUSHROOM SALAD

Although they're expensive, avocadoes are so nutritious that they're worth serving when you can. In this salad they are combined with two other high-value foods—watercress and mushrooms—to make a nutritious salad for serving at lunchtime, along with whole-grain bread, peanut butter, yeast extract, or cheese sandwiches.

Serves 2 to 4

> *1 large ripe avocado*
> *6 ounces small white button mushrooms, washed and sliced*
> *2 tablespoons lemon juice*
> *Sea salt*
> *Freshly ground black pepper*
> *A few crisp lettuce leaves*
> *1 large bunch watercress, washed*

Halve the avocado; remove the pit and skin. Cut the avocado into pieces and place in a bowl with the mushrooms. Sprinkle with lemon juice and salt and pepper to taste; mix well. Place a few lettuce leaves in the base of a large serving dish, or on individual plates. Spoon the avocado mixture on top, then arrange the watercress around the edge. Serve at once.

AVOCADO, WATERCRESS, AND WALNUT SALAD

This salad, too, is nice for lunch, with whole wheat bread and butter, or on the side, with a dish such as the Whole Wheat Pasta Rings with Tomato Sauce (page 177).

Serves 2 to 4

> *1 tablespoon wine vinegar*
> *3 tablespoons oil*
> *Sea salt*
> *Finely ground black pepper*
> *1 large ripe avocado*
> *1 large bunch watercress, washed*
> *¼ pound walnut pieces*

Put the vinegar and oil into a bowl with salt and pepper to taste and mix together. Cut the avocado in half, remove the pit and skin, and slice the flesh. Put the avocado slices into the bowl and mix gently, then add the watercress and walnuts; serve at once.

MIXED-BEAN SALAD

Serve this with some green salad, such as lettuce or watercress, and warm whole wheat rolls, for a main course.

Serves 4

> *1 tablespoon wine or cider vinegar*
> *3 tablespoons oil*
> *½ teaspoon sugar*
> *Sea salt*
> *Freshly ground black pepper*

1 cup cooked lima beans (see page 54), or one 16-ounce can, drained
1 cup cooked red kidney beans (see page 54), or one 16-ounce can, drained
2 heaping tablespoons chopped parsley
A few scallions, chopped

Put the vinegar into a large bowl or wooden salad bowl with the oil, sugar, and salt and pepper to taste; mix together. Add the beans, parsley, and scallions and stir gently.

TO FREEZE. This salad freezes well as long as you are not using beans that have already been frozen (in which case, refreezing will toughen the skins). Prepare the salad according to the recipe but do not add the parsley and scallions. Freeze. To serve, thaw completely and add the remaining ingredients. Correct the seasoning.

BEET, APPLE, AND ALFALFA SALAD

Serves 1

1 small beet, raw
1 apple
3 to 4 tablespoons orange juice
½ cup alfalfa sprouts
A few sunflower seeds, toasted (optional)

Scrub the beet and apple, then grate them both into a bowl. Add the orange juice and sprouts and mix lightly. Serve immediately.

BEET, ORANGE, AND COTTAGE CHEESE SALAD

Serves 4

> 2 *cups canned beets, drained*
> 4 *large juicy oranges*
> 1 *large bunch watercress, washed*
> 1½ *cups cottage cheese*
> 2 *to* 3 *tablespoons sunflower seeds (optional)*

Cut the beets into thin slices. Put into a bowl. Slice the skin and pith off the oranges by cutting around and around with a sharp knife, the way you would when peeling an apple if you want to keep the peel whole. Hold the oranges over the bowl of beets, to catch the juice, then slice the oranges into thin rounds. Arrange the watercress, slices of beet, slices of orange, and cottage cheese on a large serving dish or individual plates. Sprinkle with the sunflower seeds, if you're using them, and serve immediately.

IF YOU DON'T EAT DAIRY PRODUCTS. Use cooked, drained lima beans instead of the cottage cheese, or use one of the dips or spreads on pages 133–38.

BROCCOLI SALAD WITH TOMATO DRESSING

Broccoli is one of the most nutritious vegetables available, being rich in vitamins A, B, and C, along with iron and calcium, and here is a delicious and refreshing way to serve it. It's excellent with some soft whole-grain bread and white cheese or tofu spread.

Serves 2

> ¾ *pound broccoli*
> 1 *onion, peeled and chopped*

1 tablespoon oil
1 clove garlic, peeled and crushed
4 tomatoes or one 8-ounce can with liquid
Sea salt
Freshly ground black pepper

Wash and trim the broccoli. Remove only the tough stems. Cut the stems into 1-inch pieces, and separate the florets, halving or quartering the larger ones so that all are about the same size. Cook the broccoli in ¼ inch fast-boiling water until just tender, then drain, keeping the vitamin-rich liquid for soups or sauces. While the broccoli is cooking, fry the onion gently in the oil for 10 minutes, or until tender but not brown, then add the garlic and cook for a moment or two longer. Remove from the heat, add the tomatoes, and puree in a blender. Season the tomato mixture with salt and pepper to taste. Put the broccoli into a shallow dish, pour the tomato mixture over the top, and allow to stand until completely cold.

VARIATION
BROCCOLI AND YOGURT SALAD. For this creamy salad, cook the broccoli as described in the preceding recipe, then coat with a well-seasoned mixture of two-thirds thick plain yogurt and one-third mayonnaise. Spoon into a shallow dish and top with toasted slivered almonds.

CABBAGE, APPLE, AND RAISIN SALAD

Serves 4

2 cups shredded green cabbage
2 eating apples
¼ cup orange juice
¼ to ½ cup raisins
A few toasted pumpkin seeds (optional)
Thick yogurt (optional)

Shred or chop the cabbage; dice or coarsely grate the apple. Put them into a bowl with the orange juice and raisins and mix well. Some toasted pumpkin seeds are nice sprinkled over the top of this salad, and it's also good served with a dollop of thick creamy yogurt.

MAIN-COURSE CABBAGE SALAD I

This is a substantial and filling salad. Its protein is in the form of the nuts, and it makes a complete main course if you serve it with some whole wheat bread or rolls or a baked potato. You might think it would be time-consuming to make, but if you have a good chopping board and spring-loaded choppers or a food processor, it can be done quickly and can be prepared several hours in advance. It will only improve as the cabbage softens in the dressing and absorbs the flavors.

Serves 4

>*1 tablespoon wine or cider vinegar*
>*2 to 3 tablespoons oil*
>*½ teaspoon sugar*
>*Sea salt*
>*Freshly ground black pepper*
>*3 cups shredded green cabbage*
>*½ pound carrots, scraped*
>*1 small red or green pepper, deseeded*
>*1 small bunch scallions, trimmed*
>*¼ cup raisins*
>*¼ pound roasted peanuts (see page 58), or use salted ones*

Put the vinegar into a large bowl or wooden salad bowl with the oil, sugar, and salt and pepper to taste; mix together. (Don't add much salt if you're intending to use salted peanuts.) Chop the cabbage, carrots, and peppers by hand or put everything into a food processor and whizz together for a few seconds. Put the chopped vegetables into the bowl with the dressing, snip the scallions over this, using a kitchen scissors, and add the raisins. Mix everything together. Add the peanuts just before serving so that they remain crisp.

MAIN-COURSE CABBAGE SALAD II

Serves 4

> *Juice of 1 lemon*
> *2 to 3 tablespoons oil*
> *½ teaspoon sugar*
> *Sea salt*
> *Freshly ground black pepper*
> *3 cups green cabbage*
> *1 cup carrots, scraped*
> *1 red pepper, deseeded*
> *1 ripe avocado*
> *1 head lettuce*
> *1 bunch watercress*
> *4 ounces cashew nuts, roasted (see page 58), or use salted ones*

Put 1 tablespoon of the lemon juice into a large bowl and add the oil, sugar, and salt and pepper to taste; mix together. (Don't add much salt if you're intending to use salted cashews.) Chop the cabbage, carrots, and pepper by hand or put everything into a food processor and whizz together for a few seconds. Put chopped vegetables into the bowl with the dressing and mix together. Halve the avocado and remove the pit and skin. Cut the flesh into long, thin slices and sprinkle with the rest of the lemon juice. Put some crisp lettuce leaves in the base of a serving dish or on individual plates. Pile the cabbage mixture on top. Arrange the watercress and avocado slices around the edge, and top the cabbage mixture with the cashews.

CARROT, APPLE, AND CHICK-PEA SALAD

For this salad you need your own sprouted chick-peas, started 3 to 4 days beforehand. It's a super, crunchy, vitality mix.

Serves 2 to 4

> *Juice of 1 orange*
> *2 medium-size carrots, peeled and coarsely grated*
> *2 apples, diced*
> *1 to 2 cups sprouted chick-peas*

Mix everything together; serve immediately. Some chopped mint or other fresh herbs can be added, also a spoonful of natural yogurt if you like.

CARROT, APPLE, AND MINT SALAD

The fresh mint gives this salad a curiously sweet, aromatic flavor I find delicious. It is especially good with cheese dishes.

Serves 4

> *3 tablespoons oil*
> *1 tablespoon wine vinegar*
> *Sea salt*
> *Freshly ground black pepper*
> *¾ pound carrots*
> *½ pound Savoy cabbage*
> *3 sweet eating apples*
> *2 heaping tablespoons chopped fresh chives*
> *2 heaping tablespoons chopped fresh mint*

First make the dressing very simply by putting the oil and vinegar in a wooden salad bowl and mixing it with a little salt and freshly ground black pepper.

Next, scrape the carrots and dice finely; wash and shred the cabbage; dice the apples, discarding the cores. Put the carrots, cabbage, and apples into the bowl, together with the chopped chives and mint, and mix well.

SPROUTED CHICK-PEA SALAD IN PITA BREAD

Sprouted chick-peas make a wonderfully nutritious, crunchy salad lunch.

Serves 1

> *½ cup sprouted chick-peas*
> *1 small onion, peeled and sliced*
> *1 to 2 tomatoes, sliced*
> *1 tablespoon lemon juice*
> *1 tablespoon oil*
> *Sea salt*
> *Freshly ground black pepper*
> *1 whole wheat pita bread, warmed*

Mix together the chick-peas, onion, tomatoes, lemon juice, and oil. Season lightly. Spoon the mixture into the pita pocket.

CHINESE CABBAGE, TOMATO, AND SCALLION SALAD

Serves 4 to 6

> 1 pound Chinese cabbage
> 3 tablespoons oil
> 1 tablespoon wine vinegar
> Sea salt
> Freshly ground black pepper
> ½ cup chopped scallions
> 1 cup chopped tomatoes

Wash the cabbage, dry carefully, then slice. Put the oil and vinegar into a salad bowl, add salt and pepper to taste, and mix together. Add the cabbage, scallions, and tomatoes, and toss them in the dressing until everything is well coated. Serve at once.

CORN AND RADISH SALAD

Serves 4

> 1 tablespoon wine vinegar
> 3 tablespoons oil
> 2 cups cooked, drained corn
> 1 cup sliced radishes
> 1 cup chopped scallions
> Sea salt
> Freshly ground black pepper

Put the first five ingredients into a bowl and mix together thoroughly. Season with sea salt and freshly ground black pepper to taste.

GREEK SALAD

A good salad for the late summer when tomatoes and cucumbers are cheap. I like this salad with warm, light-textured whole wheat rolls. The inclusion of the parsley adds extra iron and calcium.

Serves 4

> *1 tablespoon wine vinegar*
> *3 tablespoons oil*
> *Sea salt*
> *Freshly ground black pepper*
> *1 pound firm tomatoes*
> *1 cucumber*
> *1 large mild onion, peeled*
> *2 big tablespoons chopped parsley (if available)*
> *½ pound firm white cheese: Cheshire, Caerphilly, Lancashire,*
> *or Wensleydale*
> *16 black olives (optional)*

Put the vinegar, oil, and a little seasoning into a large bowl and mix together to make a dressing. Wash and slice the tomatoes. Cut the cucumber into chunky pieces. Thinly slice the onion. Cube the cheese. Put all these, along with the olives, into the bowl with the dressing and toss them gently until evenly coated. Serve piled up attractively on individual dishes.

IF YOU DON'T EAT DAIRY PRODUCTS. Use cubes of lightly seasoned firm tofu instead of the ordinary cheese.

GREEN SALAD

Quicker than cooking a vegetable and full of vitamins, green salad is most useful. You can use any green salad vegetable, and the darker they are, the better. Watercress is excellent, also raw spinach and dark green lettuce leaves. Mix a dressing straight into the bowl: I generally use 1 tablespoon wine vinegar and 2 to 3 tablespoons cold-pressed safflower or corn oil, with some salt and pepper. Then simply put in the green vegetables, torn into pieces as necessary, or, in the case of raw spinach, finely shredded. Gently toss the vegetables in the dressing. Chopped fresh herbs, onion, and garlic can be added, and the dressing can be made more adventurous with the addition of some mustard and/or a little sugar.

RED KIDNEY BEAN SALAD

This makes a main-course salad (for lunch or a light supper), served with some watercress and warm whole wheat rolls or pita bread.

Serves 2

> 2 teaspoons wine or cider vinegar
> 1 teaspoon tomato puree
> 2 tablespoons oil
> Sugar
> Sea salt
> Freshly ground black pepper
> 1 cup cooked red kidney beans (see page 54), or one 16-ounce
>   can, drained
> 2 scallions, chopped

Put the vinegar into a large bowl or wooden salad bowl with the tomato puree, oil, and sugar, salt, and pepper to taste; mix together. Add the beans and scallions and stir gently.

TO FREEZE. This salad freezes well as long as you're not using beans that have already been frozen (in which case, refreezing will toughen the skins). Prepare the salad according to the recipe, but do not add the scallions. Freeze. To serve, thaw completely, and add the remaining ingredient. Correct the seasoning.

HOT POTATO SALAD WITH PEANUT DRESSING

This is one of those dishes that sound very strange but taste really good. It's a mixture of hot and cold, bland and spicy, and it is rich in protein too. You can use ordinary salted peanuts but if you can get the plain roasted kind, they're better.

Serves 4

> *2 cups roasted unsalted peanuts*
> *⅔ cup milk*
> *½ cup finely grated cheddar cheese*
> *½ to 1 teaspoon chili powder, or 1 small green chili*
> *1½ pounds potatoes*
> *1 head lettuce*
> *1 bunch watercress*
> *4 tomatoes*
> *1 onion*

Place the peanuts and milk in a blender and blend until thick and fairly smooth (add a little more milk if necessary to give the consistency of whipped cream). Turn the mixture into a bowl and stir in the grated cheese. Add chili powder to taste. Or, if you're using a fresh chili, remove and discard the seeds and chop the flesh very finely, then add it to the mixture a little at a time, tasting to get the right degree of hotness.

Cut the potatoes into walnut-size pieces, then boil them until they're just tender; drain. Wash the lettuce, watercress, and tomatoes; peel the onion. Slice the onion and tomatoes into thin rounds.

To serve, spoon the hot potatoes into the center of a serving dish (or individual plates) and arrange the lettuce, watercress, tomatoes, and onion around the edge. Spoon the peanut sauce over the potatoes and serve at once.

RICE AND ARTICHOKE-HEART SALAD

This makes a complete meal if you serve it with a soup or one or two other vegetable salads, such as a bowl of crisp lettuce and herbs or a juicy tomato salad. A green salad with Gruyère cheese or the tomato salad with cheese and olives will supply the extra protein needed; or the salad can be garnished with wedges of hard-boiled egg. Alternatively, you could start or end the meal with a protein dish, such as a lentil soup or homemade ice cream.

Serves 4

> 1¼ cups long-grain brown rice
> 2½ cups water
> Sea salt
> 14 ounces canned artichoke hearts, drained
> 1 clove garlic
> 1 tablespoon wine vinegar
> 3 tablespoons oil
> Freshly ground black pepper
> Chopped parsley
> 1 tablespoon chopped fresh chives
> 3 hard-boiled eggs, peeled and quartered (optional)

Put the rice into a heavy-based saucepan with the water and ½ teaspoon of the salt. Bring to a boil, reduce the heat, and cook very gently for 40 to 45 minutes, or until the rice is tender and all the water has been absorbed. If there is still a little water, put the lid back on the saucepan and leave it to stand (off the heat) for 10 to 15 minutes.

While the rice is cooking slice the artichoke hearts. Peel and crush the garlic in a little salt with the blade of a knife. Dice the garlic and mix it in a small bowl with the vinegar, oil, and a grinding of pepper. Stir this mixture gently into the hot rice, together with 1 tablespoon of the parsley, the chives, and the sliced artichoke hearts, using a fork to avoid mashing the rice. Check the seasoning, then leave the mixture to cool at room temperature.

Serve the salad in a shallow dish garnished with additional chopped parsley and the hard-boiled eggs, if you're using them, tucked around the edge.

SOYBEAN SALAD

Soybeans are so nutritious, being rich in iron and thiamine and containing useful amounts of calcium, that it's worth finding a number of different ways of serving them. Here they're mixed with carrots, parsley, and scallions to make a very nourishing salad.

Serves 4

> *1 teaspoon turbinado sugar*
> *1 teaspoon dry mustard*
> *Sea salt*
> *2 tablespoons wine or cider vinegar*
> *3 tablespoons oil*
> *2 cups cooked soybeans (see page 54) or soybean sprouts (see page 111)*
> *3 large carrots, coarsely grated*
> *1 small bunch scallions, trimmed and chopped*
> *2 heaping tablespoons chopped parsley*
> *Soy sauce (optional)*

Put the sugar and mustard into a bowl with a little salt and mix to a paste with the vinegar. Then gradually add the oil. Stir in the soybeans, or soybean sprouts, the carrots, scallions, and parsley. Taste, and add a little more salt if necessary. A few drops of soy sauce are nice in this, too.

SPINACH SALAD

Uncooked spinach is an excellent source of iron, vitamin C, and folic acid, and this is one of my favorite salads. I even get cravings for it if I'm a bit tired or run down. It can be served as a side salad, though I prefer it on its own, as a cleansing lunch or supper. You could add some sprouted seeds (see page 111) or scatter some pumpkin seeds, sesame seeds, or savory seed mix (see pages 186–87) on top for protein, if you like.

Serves 4

> *1 tablespoon wine vinegar*
> *2 to 3 tablespoons oil*
> *1 pound spinach, washed and shredded as finely as possible*
> *2 leeks, about 10 ounces together, washed, trimmed, and finely*
> *shredded (use as much of the green part as is reasonably*
> *tender)*
> *Sea salt*
> *Freshly ground pepper*
> *Soy sauce (optional)*

Put the vinegar and oil into a salad bowl and mix together. Add the spinach and leeks and mix gently. Season with salt and pepper to taste and serve at once. A few drops of soy sauce are nice in this, too.

GRATED RUTABAGA SALAD

A delicious, creamy salad that's rich in B vitamins.

Serves 4

>   *1 pound grated raw rutabaga*
>   *2 heaping tablespoons mayonnaise*
>   *3 heaping tablespoons plain yogurt*
>   *Sea salt*
>   *Freshly ground black pepper*
>   *1 bunch watercress, washed and trimmed*
>   *4 tomatoes, sliced*
>   *¼ pound home-grown sprouted mung beans (if available)*

Mix together the rutabaga, mayonnaise, and yogurt. Season with salt and pepper to taste; spoon into a large dish. Tuck the watercress all round the edge of the rutabaga mixture, then arrange the tomato slices on top, and finally sprinkle with the sprouted mung beans.

IF YOU DON'T EAT DAIRY PRODUCTS. Use an eggless mayonnaise.

TABBOULEH

A useful salad, because it's a good way of eating a lot of parsley, which is a very good source of both calcium and iron. Serve as a main salad course, with some crisp lettuce leaves on the side and perhaps some Yogurt Dressing (page 109).

Serves 4

> 1 cup bulgur
> 2 cups boiling water
> 3 tablespoons oil
> 1 tablespoon lemon juice
> 1 cup chopped parsley
> 2 tomatoes, skinned and finely chopped
> 2 tablespoons chopped mint
> Sea salt
> Freshly ground black pepper
> Extra oil to serve (optional)

Put the bulgur into a bowl, cover with the boiling water, and leave to soak for 15 minutes. If the bulgur has not absorbed the water completely, drain off the excess. Add the oil, lemon juice, parsley, tomatoes, and mint to the wheat, and salt and pepper to taste; mix well. Spoon the salad onto a shallow serving dish, level the top, and press down to make a flat cakelike shape. Chill. Spoon a little extra oil on top before serving, if liked.

VITALITY SALAD BOWL

This is pleasant spooned into a warm pita bread pocket and topped with some mayonnaise or tofu dressing and a sprinkling of watercress.

Serves 4

> 1 tablespoon wine or cider vinegar
> 1 tablespoon oil
> Sea salt
> Freshly ground black pepper
> ½ cup wheat berries, soaked overnight, then cooked for 1¼ hours (or 25 minutes in a pressure cooker) or 1 cup sprouted wheat
> 1 cup any kind home-grown bean sprouts
> 2 carrots, scraped and coarsely grated
> 2 ounces raisins
> 4 tomatoes, diced
> 4 inch cucumber, peeled and diced
> 2 stalks celery, sliced

Put the vinegar and oil into a bowl. Season with salt and pepper to taste; mix. Add the cooked grain or sprouted wheat, bean sprouts, carrots, raisins, tomatoes, cucumber, and celery, and toss gently so that they all get coated with the dressing.

Sandwiches, Dips, and Spreads

Here are some ideas for sandwiches, including ones that can be made in advance and kept in the freezer until required. If you are going to store them in the freezer, use fresh ingredients (not from the freezer): Use not-previously-frozen whole-grain bread, rolls, or pita bread, the Whole Wheat Scones with Molasses on page 228, or the Apricot, Almond, and Wheat Germ Loaf on page 221. Butter lightly, and spread with your choice of fillings, avoiding salad ingredients and hard-boiled eggs, which do not freeze well. Sandwiches will keep in the freezer for 3 to 4 weeks.

Add a container of yogurt or one of the cakes on pages 222–27 and some fresh fruit to complete the meal.

Here are some ideas:

SWEET SANDWICH FILLINGS

- . . . Honey mixed with finely grated nuts
- . . . Cottage or farmer cheese with chopped crystallized ginger
- . . . Cottage or farmer cheese with chopped "canned in its own juice" pineapple
- . . . Dates softened by heating in a little water, then beaten smooth
- . . . Peanut butter or Peanut-Pumpkin Spread and sliced banana (don't freeze)
- . . . Softened dates with chopped nuts added or some cottage or farmer cheese beaten in

SAVORY SANDWICH FILLINGS AND LUNCH-BOX FILLERS

- · · · Slice of cold nut, lentil, or soybean loaf with chutney
- · · · Hazelnut and Vegetable Pasties (page 152)
- · · · Soy Sausages (page 159) with pickle in a soft whole wheat roll
- · · · Grated cheese or vegan cheese with pickle
- · · · Any of the dips or spreads below
- · · · Cooked beans in a little oil and vinegar dressing
- · · · Mixed-Bean Salad (page 114) in a pocket of pita bread
- · · · Peanut butter or Peanut-Pumpkin Spread (page 137) with finely grated carrot (don't freeze)
- · · · Cabbage, Apple, and Raisin Salad (page 117) in a pocket of pita bread (don't freeze)
- · · · Vitality Salad Bowl (page 131) in a pocket of pita bread (don't freeze)
- · · · Greek Salad (page 123) in pita bread (don't freeze)
- · · · Sprouted or cooked chick-peas or soybeans with grated carrot and finely chopped scallion, mixed with some mayonnaise, thick yogurt, or Tofu Dressing (page 110) in pita bread (don't freeze)

SPREADS

BEAN SPREAD

Makes about 1½ cups

> *1½ cups cooked lima beans or one 16-ounce can, with liquid*
> *1 clove garlic, peeled and crushed*
> *1 tablespoon olive oil*
> *2 teaspoons wine vinegar*
> *A few drops of Tabasco sauce or a pinch of cayenne*
> *Sea salt*
> *Freshly ground black pepper*

Drain the beans, keeping the liquid. Mash the beans and add the garlic, oil, vinegar, and enough of the reserved cooking or canning liquid to make a consistency like softly whipped cream; or puree in a blender or food processor. Add the Tabasco or cayenne and salt and pepper to taste. Spoon into a small container.

TO FREEZE. Leave out the garlic and Tabasco or cayenne. Put the spread into a small container, cover, and freeze. Remove from the freezer 2 hours in advance. Spices can be added before use.

CHEESE SPREAD

Makes about 1½ cups

> 3 tablespoons margarine, softened
> 1¼ cups grated Cheddar cheese
> 6 tablespoons milk
> Pinch of cayenne or a few drops of Tabasco sauce
> Sea salt
> Freshly ground black pepper

Put all the ingredients into food processor and blend to a creamy consistency. Or put the margarine into a bowl and beat until soft, then gradually beat in the cheese and milk. Season with cayenne or Tabasco and salt and pepper to taste. Spoon into a small dish or container.

IF YOU DON'T EAT DAIRY PRODUCTS. Use Vegan Cheese (page 138) and soy milk.

TO FREEZE. Cover the dish with plastic wrap and freeze. Remove from the freezer 2 hours before required.

HUMMUS

Makes about 1¾ cups

> 1½ cups cooked chick-peas or one 16-ounce can, with liquid
> 1 clove garlic, peeled and crushed
> 2 tablespoons tahini
> 2 tablespoons olive oil
> 1 tablespoon lemon juice
> Sea salt
> Freshly ground black pepper

Make in the same way as Bean Spread, above, adding the tahini and lemon juice along with the oil and beating in enough cooking liquid to make a soft consistency.

TO FREEZE. Same for Bean Spread, above.

LENTIL SPREAD

Makes about 1¼ cups

> ½ cup split red lentils
> 1 cup water
> 1 small onion, peeled and finely chopped
> 2 tablespoons butter
> 2 teaspoons curry powder or a little yeast extract
> Sea salt
> Freshly ground black pepper

Wash the lentils and cook them in the water for 20 to 30 minutes, or until they're tender and have absorbed all the water. Mash them roughly with a fork. Fry the onion in the butter until tender, then add the curry powder, if you're using this, and fry for 1 to 2 minutes more.

Blend this mixture into the lentils to make a fairly smooth paste. Season to taste, adding the yeast extract at this point, if you're flavoring with this. Let cool before using.

VARIATION
For Lentil and Mushroom Spread, fry 1 cup finely chopped mushrooms along with the onion. Continue to fry until any liquid has evaporated. Omit the curry powder. Add the cooked lentils and season with yeast extract, salt, and pepper. This is a particularly nutritious spread, being rich in B vitamins and iron.

TO FREEZE. Not ideal for freezing because of the curry powder, which can develop a musty flavor, but if you want to risk it, freeze as for Bean Spread, for not more than 3 to 4 weeks.

HAZELNUT SPREAD

Makes about 1½ cups

> ¾ *cup hazelnuts*
> ¾ *cup sunflower seeds*
> 2 *tablespoons margarine*
> ¼ *cup hot water*
> 1 *clove garlic, peeled and crushed*
> 1 *tablespoon soy sauce*
> *Sea salt*
> *Freshly ground black pepper*

Toast the nuts and seeds under the broiler or in a moderate oven until golden brown, about 10 to 15 minutes. If the nuts still have brown skins on, rub these off after toasting by rubbing the nuts gently in a clean soft cloth. Grind the nuts and seeds finely in a coffee grinder or blender. Mix this with the margarine, water, garlic, and soy sauce. Beat until smooth and creamy. Season with salt and pepper to taste. Spoon into a small dish.

PEANUT-PUMPKIN SPREAD

Makes just over ½ cup

> ¼ cup peanuts
> ¼ cup pumpkin seeds
> ⅛ to ¼ cup oil

Preheat the oven to 375°F. Spread out the peanuts and pumpkin seeds on a ungreased baking sheet and roast in the oven for 10 to 15 minutes, or until golden brown. Grind the nuts and pumpkin seeds to a powder in a food processor or blender, then add enough oil to make a spreading consistency.

CURRIED SOYBEAN AND APPLE SPREAD

Makes about 1½ cups

> 1 small onion, peeled and finely chopped
> 2 tablespoons margarine
> 1 medium-size cooking apple, cored and finely chopped
> 1 tablespoon curry powder
> 1 cup cooked soybeans
> Sea salt
> Freshly ground black pepper

Fry the onion in the margarine for 5 minutes, then add the apple and curry powder. Fry, covered, for 5 minutes more, or until the onion and apple are soft. Remove from the heat and add the soybeans. Mash well, adding a little water if necessary to make a soft consistency (use the water in which the beans were cooked, if you have it). Season with salt and pepper to taste. Spoon the mixture into a small container.

TO FREEZE. Not ideal for freezing because of the curry powder, which can develop a musty flavor, but if you want to risk it, freeze as for Bean Spread, for not more than 3 to 4 weeks.

TOFU SPREAD

This is an easy and delicious spread that babies love; it makes an excellent vegan replacement for cottage cheese in salads and sandwiches.

Makes just over 1 cup

> 1 cup firm tofu, mashed
> 1 to 2 cloves garlic, peeled and crushed
> 4 teaspoons fresh chopped herbs
> Sea salt
> Freshly ground black pepper

Add the garlic and herbs to the tofu. Season lightly (this will be unnecessary for babies). You can use a blender for a smoother, more cohesive result.

VEGAN CHEESE

Makes 1 cup

> ¼ pound (1 stick) hard soy margarine
> 1 teaspoon yeast extract
> ½ cup soy flour
> Sea salt
> Freshly ground black pepper

Put the margarine and yeast extract into a saucepan and heat until melted. Remove from heat and stir in the soy flour and salt and pepper to taste. Pour the mixture into a small dish or suitable mold, such as a small plastic container. Let cool, then chill until firm. Can be sliced or grated and used as a replacement for dairy cheese.

TO FREEZE. Cover the dish with plastic wrap and freeze. Remove from the freezer 2 hours before required.

Freezer Dishes

SAUCES FOR THE FREEZER

VEGETARIAN GRAVY

Makes just over 3 cups

> *1 onion, peeled and chopped*
> *3 tablespoons oil*
> *2 tablespoons flour (I use an 85 percent whole wheat)*
> *1 clove garlic, peeled and crushed*
> *3 cups water*
> *1 cube vegetable bouillon (optional)*
> *2 teaspoons yeast extract*
> *1 tablespoon soy sauce*
> *Sea salt*
> *Freshly ground black pepper*

Fry the onion in the oil for 10 minutes. Add the flour and let it brown over the heat for 5 to 10 minutes, stirring all the time. Then add all the remaining ingredients. Bring to a boil and simmer for 10 minutes. Then strain and correct the seasoning. If you like bits of onion in your gravy, there's no need to strain; in this case you could use a 100 percent flour instead of the one suggested. (There's no point in using the 100 percent flour if you're going to strain the gravy because the bran will get left in the sieve anyway.)

WHITE SAUCE AND VARIATIONS

These ingredients double up satisfactorily if you want to make a larger quantity, but you'll need a big saucepan. I like to use unbleached white flour from the health food store, since it's free from chemicals and additives, but ordinary plain flour would also do.

Makes 2 cups

> 4 tablespoons (½ stick) butter or margarine
> ¼ cup unbleached white flour
> 2 cups milk or soy milk
> 1 bay leaf
> Sea salt
> Freshly ground black pepper

For the traditional method, melt the butter or margarine, then stir in flour. Cook for 1 minute, then add one-third of the milk and stir until thickened; repeat with another third, then finally add the rest, together with the bay leaf and seasoning. Or put all the ingredients into a saucepan and whisk together over moderate heat until thickened. Or puree the butter or margarine, flour, and milk in a blender for 1 minute, then pour into a saucepan and stir over moderate heat until thickened. In all cases, simmer gently for 10 minutes to cook the flour, then season.

VARIATIONS

ALMOND SAUCE. Stir ½ to 1 cup ground almonds and some grated nutmeg or a small grated onion into the cooked sauce. A little extra milk may be needed to bring the sauce back to the right consistency.

PARSLEY SAUCE. Add 2 heaping tablespoons chopped parsley (or more—parsley is a wonderful source of calcium and iron) to the cooked sauce.

CHEESE SAUCE. Stir ½ to 1 cup grated Cheddar cheese and a pinch of dry mustard powder or cayenne into the cooked sauce.

TO FREEZE. Pour the sauce into a suitable covered container, allowing enough room for the sauce to expand as it freezes. To serve, remove from the freezer and allow to thaw for about 2 hours. Stir gently over heat.

TOMATO SAUCE

Makes 1½ cups

> 1 onion, peeled and chopped
> 2 tablespoons oil
> One 16-ounce can tomatoes, with liquid
> Sea salt
> Freshly ground black pepper

Fry the onion in the oil for 10 minutes, or until soft. Remove from the heat, add the tomatoes, and puree in a blender—no further cooking is needed. Season with salt and pepper to taste.

TO FREEZE. Pour into a suitable covered container, allowing room for the sauce to expand as it freezes. To serve, allow up to 2 hours for the sauce to defrost.

FREEZER SAVORIES

ASPARAGUS CROUSTADE

Make and freeze the base, then add the topping later. For a less expensive, but equally nutritious version, broccoli can be used instead, or a mixture of half broccoli and half fried button mushrooms.

Serves 6

> *FOR THE BASE*
> 1 cup mixed almonds and Brazil nuts, grated
> 1 cup slivered almonds

¾ cup soft whole wheat bread crumbs
1 onion, peeled and finely grated
2 cloves garlic, peeled and crushed
½ teaspoon mixed herbs
¼ pound (1 stick) butter, softened
Sea salt
Freshly ground black pepper

FOR THE TOPPING
2 pounds asparagus
One 16-ounce container sour cream
Sea salt
Freshly ground black pepper
A few extra slivered almonds

Heat the oven to 450°F. Put the grated and slivered nuts in a bowl along with the bread crumbs, onion, garlic, and mixed herbs. Add the butter, mixing with a fork until well combined. Season with salt and pepper to taste. Press the mixture firmly into the base of a shallow 12-inch quiche or pizza pan. Bake for about 10 minutes, or until crisp. Let cool.

To prepare the topping, cut the tough ends off the asparagus; wash asparagus well. Cook the asparagus in 1 inch of boiling water in a large saucepan for 10 to 15 minutes, or until tender. Drain. Arrange the asparagus on top of the nutty base. Mix the sour cream with a little salt and pepper, then pour over the asparagus, so that it is nearly all covered. Sprinkle with a few slivered almonds. Return to the oven for 5 to 10 minutes, just to heat through the cream. Serve immediately.

IF YOU DON'T EAT DAIRY PRODUCTS. Use a soy margarine instead of the butter and 2 cups White Sauce (page 140) made from soy milk instead of the sour cream.

TO FREEZE. Let the base cool, then wrap it carefully and freeze it in the pan. To serve, thaw, then heat thoroughly (about 15 to 20 minutes) in a moderate oven. Make the topping as described above. Frozen asparagus can be used; you'll need 1 pound.

BROCCOLI IN CHEESE OR ALMOND SAUCE

Serve this nice, easygoing dish with crunchy baked potatoes and a tomato salad.

Serves 4 to 5

> 2 pounds broccoli
> 4 tablespoons (½ stick) butter or margarine
> ¼ cup flour
> 2 cups milk
> ½ cup grated sharp cheese or ¼ cup ground almonds and a
>   grated onion
> Grated rind of ½ lemon
> Sea salt
> Freshly ground black pepper
> Crisp whole-grain bread crumbs
> ⅓ cup slivered or chopped almonds

Trim and wash the broccoli, removing only the coarser stems. Cut the stems into 1-inch pieces; break the florets into small sections, halving or quartering any larger ones. Cook in ½ inch fast-boiling water until just tender, about 5 minutes; drain well, keeping the vitamin-rich liquid for soups or sauces. If you're serving this immediately, heat the broiler.

To make the sauce: Melt the butter or margarine, stir in the flour, and cook for a minute or two. Then gradually stir in the milk until thickened. Simmer the sauce over a very gentle heat for 5 minutes. Remove from the heat, add half the grated cheese or all the ground almonds and the grated onion. Season with the lemon rind and salt and pepper to taste. Put the broccoli into a shallow gratin dish. Pour the sauce over the top. Sprinkle with bread crumbs, the rest of the cheese (if you're using this), and the almonds. Heat under the broiler for 5 to 10 minutes, or until the top is golden and crisp.

TO FREEZE. Sprinkle the top with the bread crumbs, cheese, and almonds, as above. Let cool completely, wrap well, and freeze. To serve, thaw, then bake in a moderate oven (400°F) for 30 to 40 minutes.

BROCCOLI AND TOMATO AU GRATIN

Serves 4

> *1½ pounds broccoli*
> *1 large onion, peeled and chopped*
> *1 tablespoon oil*
> *1 clove garlic, crushed*
> *1 pound tomatoes, skinned and quartered, or one 16-ounce can,*
> * with liquid*
> *Sea salt*
> *Freshly ground black pepper*
> *¼ cup dried whole wheat bread crumbs*
> *½ cup grated Cheddar cheese*

Preheat the oven to 400°F. Prepare the broccoli exactly as in the previous recipe. While the broccoli is cooking, gently fry the onion in the oil for 10 minutes, or until tender but not brown, then add the garlic and cook for a moment or two longer. Remove from the heat, add the tomatoes, and puree in a blender. Season the tomato mixture with salt and pepper to taste. Put the broccoli into a shallow ovenproof dish and pour the tomato mixture over the top. Sprinkle with the dried crumbs and grated cheese. Bake for 30 minutes, or until the inside is piping hot and cheese is melted and lightly browned.

IF YOU DON'T EAT DAIRY PRODUCTS. Sprinkle the top of the gratin with ¼ cup grated hazelnuts or sunflower seeds and top with 4 teaspoons margarine, dotted over the surface.

TO FREEZE. Make up the complete dish, but don't bake in the oven. Let cool, wrap, and freeze. To use, allow 3 to 4 hours to thaw, then bake as above.

KASHA BAKE

Like the other grains, kasha, or buckwheat groats, is rich in iron and B vitamins. It also contains a substance called rutin, which naturopaths prescribe for high blood pressure and varicose veins. Serve with a lettuce or watercress salad.

Serves 4 to 6

> 6 ounces roasted kasha
> 1½ cups hot water
> 1 teaspoon yeast extract
> 1 teaspoon salt
> 2 tablespoons butter or margarine
> 1 large onion, peeled and chopped
> 3 carrots, scraped and sliced
> 2 leeks, washed and sliced
> 1 cup button mushrooms, washed and sliced
> 1 cup tomatoes, skinned and sliced
> 1 cup cooked cannellini (white kidney beans), drained, or one
>   16-ounce can, drained
> Freshly ground black pepper
>
> *FOR TOPPING*
> 1 tablespoon flour
> 1¼ cups plain yogurt
> 1 egg

If you're going to serve this immediately, preheat the oven to 375°F; there's no need to do this if you're cooking for the freezer. Grease a shallow ovenproof dish. Put the kasha into a saucepan with the hot water, yeast extract, and a little salt. Bring to a boil, stir, cover, reduce the heat, and cook for 10 minutes, or until the grain is fluffy and all the water absorbed. Meanwhile, melt the butter or margarine in a saucepan and fry the onion, carrots, and leeks gently, covered, for 7 minutes. Add the mushrooms and tomatoes and cook for 3 minutes more, then add the beans. Season with pepper to taste. Put half the kasha into the casserole dish, spoon the vegetables over, and top with the rest of the grain.

To make the topping: Whisk together the flour, yogurt, and egg. Season and pour over the top of the bake. Bake for 30 minutes.

IF YOU DON'T EAT DAIRY PRODUCTS. For the topping, omit the egg; use Vegan Yogurt (page 219) and 2 tablespoons flour.

TO FREEZE. Assemble the casserole without the topping. Wrap well in plastic and freeze. To serve, thaw for 3 to 4 hours; cover with the topping and bake as above.

LIMA BEAN AND VEGETABLE CASSEROLE

Serve this with baked potatoes or some cooked brown rice or kasha.

Serves 4

>2 large onions, peeled and chopped
>3 tablespoons oil
>2 pounds mixed root vegetables (carrot, rutabaga, parsnip, turnip, celery, as available), cut into even-size pieces
>2 tablespoons 85 percent flour
>1 cup dried lima beans, soaked for 6 to 8 hours in cold water, then drained and rinsed
>3 cups water
>2 cubes vegetable bouillon
>1 to 2 tablespoons soy sauce
>Sea salt
>Freshly ground black pepper
>Chopped parsley

Fry the onion in the oil over moderate heat for 5 minutes, then add the vegetables and stir for a minute or two. Sprinkle in the flour and mix with the vegetables, then add the beans, water, and stock cubes. Cover and simmer gently for 1½ to 2 hours, or until the vegetables and beans are tender; or bake, covered, at 325°F for 2 hours. Add the soy sauce and season with salt and pepper to taste.

TO SERVE IMMEDIATELY. Sprinkle with the chopped parsley.

TO FREEZE. Cook as above, undercooking the vegetables and beans slightly. Let it cool quickly. Put into a rigid covered container, allowing enough room for expansion. To serve, allow to defrost for 6 hours or overnight. Transfer to a saucepan and stir over gentle heat. Or transfer to a casserole dish and bake as described above for 30 to 40 minutes, or until heated through.

CARROT SLICES

These freeze well and are pleasant with Parsley Sauce (page 141) and vegetables or a salad. They also contain oats, which are a useful traditional remedy for "baby blues."

Serves 4

> 1¾ cups rolled oats
> 1 cup finely grated carrot
> 1 cup grated Cheddar cheese
> 1 egg, beaten
> 4 tablespoons (½ stick) margarine, melted
> Sea salt
> Freshly ground black pepper

Grease an 8-by-12-inch jelly roll pan. Put the oats, carrot, cheese, egg, and margarine into a bowl and mix together. Season to taste, then press into the pan.

TO SERVE IMMEDIATELY. Bake for about 20 minutes at 375°F, or until set and lightly browned.

IF YOU DON'T EAT DAIRY PRODUCTS. Use Vegan Cheese (page 138) instead of dairy cheese and 1 tablespoon soy flour mixed with 3 tablespoons water instead of egg.

TO FREEZE. Bake for 10 minutes, let cool, wrap well, and freeze. To serve, allow to thaw for 2 to 3 hours, then bake at the same temperature for 15 to 20 minutes.

CHEESE FRITTERS

These are a bit fiddly to make, but are a useful standby to have in the freezer because all the children of my acquaintance adore them and they can be fried when still frozen, making them invaluable for quick meals. When I'm making a batch for the freezer, I find that doubling the recipe makes a convenient quantity to handle.

Serves 4 to 6

> *1 clove*
> *1 onion, peeled*
> *1 bay leaf*
> *2 cups milk*
> *⅔ scant cup semolina*
> *1 cup grated Cheddar cheese*
> *2 tablespoons chopped parsley*
> *1 teaspoon dry mustard*
> *1 teaspoon sea salt*
> *Freshly ground black pepper to taste*
> *1 egg, beaten*
> *1 cup crisp whole-grain bread crumbs to coat*
> *Olive oil for shallow frying*
> *Sliced lemon for garnish*

Stick the clove into the onion and put it into a saucepan with the bay leaf and milk. Bring the milk to a boil, cover, and remove from the heat. Let stand for 10 to 15 minutes to extract the flavors. Remove the onion and bay leaf. Bring the milk back to a boil, then sprinkle the semolina on top gradually, stirring all the time. Let the mixture cook gently for 5 to 10 minutes, then remove from the heat and stir in the cheese, parsley, and seasoning. Spread the mixture out on a large plate or tray so that it is ½ inch deep. Leave until completely cold. The mixture will then be firm enough to handle. Cut into rectangular or triangular pieces; dip in the beaten egg and bread crumbs to coat thoroughly.

TO SERVE IMMEDIATELY. Pour olive oil into a skillet to equal ¼ inch and fry the fritters over a moderate heat for 3 to 4 minutes on each side, or until crisp and golden brown; drain well on paper towels. They're good with Parsley Sauce (page 141) or Yogurt Dressing (page 109).

IF YOU DON'T EAT DAIRY PRODUCTS. Use a fortified soy milk instead of dairy milk, crumbled tofu instead of grated cheese, and a thin paste made from chick-pea flour and water instead of beaten egg. Flavor with a little yeast extract.

TO FREEZE. Freeze the fritters after coating with bread crumbs but before frying. Put them on an open tray or baking tin and freeze until firm, then pack in a plastic bag or other suitable container. To serve, take right from the freezer and fry as above.

CHUNKY NUT AND VEGETABLE ROAST

This nut roast has a pleasant, chewy texture. If you're making it for a baby to share, however, it would be better to grind the nuts and chop the vegetables more finely.

Serves 4 to 6

> 1 *carrot, scraped*
> 1 *onion, peeled*
> 1 *stalk celery*
> 2 *cups mixed nuts (for instance almonds, peanuts, Brazil nuts)*
> 2 *teaspoons yeast extract*
> 2 *eggs*
> 1 *to 2 teaspoons mixed dried herbs*
> *Sea salt*
> *Freshly ground black pepper*
> *Butter and dried bread crumbs (see page 55) for coating loaf*
> *pan*

Preheat the oven to 375°F. Put all the ingredients except the butter and crumbs into a food processor and process until the vegetables and nuts are chopped into chunky pieces. Or spread the vegetables and nuts out on a large board and chop by hand, then put into a bowl and mix with the remaining ingredients. Line a 1-pound loaf pan with a strip of wax paper. Grease well and sprinkle with crumbs. Spoon the nut mixture into the pan and level top. Bake, uncovered, for 45 minutes, or until the center is set.

TO SERVE IMMEDIATELY. Slip a knife around the edge and turn the loaf out onto a warm serving dish. It's good with Vegetarian Gravy (page 140) and cooked vegetables, or cold with Yogurt Dressing (page 109) and salad.

IF YOU DON'T EAT DAIRY PRODUCTS. Replace the eggs with 2 tablespoons soy flour and 6 tablespoons water.

TO FREEZE. Bake for 20 minutes, cool quickly, wrap well and freeze. To serve, allow to thaw for 3 to 4 hours, then bake at the same temperature for 25 to 30 minutes.

HAZELNUT AND VEGETABLE PASTIES

These are particularly useful as a lunch-box item. Other nuts can be used instead of the hazelnuts—roasted peanuts are good. If you're making this for a baby, finely grate the nuts and serve only the cooked filling; the baby doesn't need pastry.

Makes 4

> 1 onion, peeled and chopped
> 2 tablespoons oil
> ½ pound potatoes, peeled and cut into ¼-inch dice
> ½ pound carrots, scraped and cut into ¼-inch dice
> 1 tablespoon tomato puree
> 1 teaspoon dried basil
> 1 cup skinned hazelnuts, chopped
> Sea salt
> Freshly ground black pepper
> 1½ cups whole wheat pastry made from 1½ cups (packed) 100
>   percent whole wheat flour, ¼ pound (1 stick) margarine, and
>   3 tablespoons cold water

Fry the onion in the oil for 5 minutes, then add the potatoes and carrots. Cover and cook gently over low heat for 10 to 15 minutes, or until the vegetables are just tender, stirring often. Add the tomato puree, basil, and hazelnuts; season with salt and pepper to taste. Set aside to cool while you make the pastry.

    Preheat the oven to 400°F. Divide the pastry into 4 pieces; roll each into a circle 6 inches across. Spoon a quarter of the vegetable mixture onto the center, fold up the pastry, and press the edges together, like a Cornish pastie. Make steam holes and bake for 20 to 25 minutes.

TO FREEZE. This can be frozen before or after cooking. If freezing before cooking, don't make steam holes, as the liquid will expand and flow out. To serve, thaw for 3 to 4 hours. If the pasties were frozen after being baked, they can be used immediately upon thawing or heated through gently for about 10 minutes in a moderate oven. For unbaked pasties, make steam holes, then bake as described above.

LEEK AND POTATO PIE

In the summer this can be made with zucchini instead of leeks, sliced and very lightly cooked in a little boiling water until just tender.

Serves 4

> *1½ pounds potatoes, peeled and cut into walnut-size chunks*
> *1½ pounds leeks, trimmed, washed, and sliced*
> *4 tablespoons (½ stick) butter or margarine*
> *2 cups milk or soy milk*
> *½ cup unbleached white flour*
> *Sea salt*
> *Freshly ground black pepper*
> *2 heaping tablespoons chopped parsley*
> *½ cup grated Cheddar cheese*

Preheat the oven to 400°F. Boil the potatoes in water to cover until tender, then drain and mash with 1 tablespoon of the butter or margarine and ½ cup of the milk; season with salt and pepper to taste. Boil the leeks in 1 inch lightly salted water for 5 to 7 minutes, or until tender; drain well. While the vegetables are cooking, make the sauce: Melt the remaining 3 tablespoons butter or margarine in a saucepan, slowly add the flour and the remaining 1½ cups milk and whisk together over moderate heat for 2 to 3 minutes, or until thickened, then simmer gently for 10 minutes. Add the drained leeks and parsley and season to taste. Spoon this mixture into a shallow ovenproof dish and spread the mashed potato evenly over the top. Sprinkle with the cheese.

TO SERVE IMMEDIATELY. Bake for 40 minutes.

IF YOU DON'T EAT DAIRY PRODUCTS. Use Vegan Cheese (page 138) instead of dairy cheese.

TO FREEZE. Freeze the pie before baking. To serve, allow to thaw for 5 to 6 hours or overnight, then bake as above.

LENTIL ENCHILADAS

Lentils are an excellent source of iron. This recipe makes a large batch of enchiladas, for the freezer.

Makes 28 to 30

> *2 cups split red lentils*
> *4 cups water*
> *4 bay leaves*
> *3 large onions, peeled and finely chopped*
> *2 red or green peppers, deseeded and finely chopped*
> *2 cloves garlic, peeled and crushed*
> *1 heaping tablespoon grated peeled fresh ginger*
> *¼ cup oil*
> *3 to 4 tablespoons lemon juice*
> *¼ cup tomato puree*
> *Sea salt*
> *Freshly ground black pepper*
> *¾ to 1 cup whole wheat flour for coating*
> *Oil for shallow frying*

Put the lentils into a pan with the water and bay leaves. Bring to a boil, then cover and reduce the heat. Cook very gently for 15 to 20 minutes, or until the lentils are soft and pale-colored and all the liquid has been absorbed; remove the bay leaf. Meanwhile, fry the onions, peppers, garlic, and ginger in the oil over medium heat for 10 minutes, or until softened. Remove from the heat and add the lentils; mix well, mashing the lentils as you do so. Add the lemon juice, tomato puree, and salt and pepper to taste. Form into flat cakes—don't make them too big if you want to use them straight from the freezer—and coat with whole wheat flour.

TO SERVE IMMEDIATELY. Shallow-fry in a little oil, treating them gently, since they're rather fragile. They're good with the Yogurt Dressing (page 109) and a salad, or gravy, mint sauce, and cooked vegetables.

TO FREEZE. Put the enchiladas on a large plate or baking tray and freeze, uncovered, until solid. Then put them into a plastic bag or container. They can be used frozen as long as you cook them gently to allow time for the center to cook through. Or allow to thaw for about 2 hours, then fry.

LENTIL LOAF

This is another recipe that is unfailingly popular with all the children of my acquaintance, probably because of its delicate flavor. My young daughter likes it smothered with mint sauce and, preferably, accompanied by crisp roast potatoes.

> ⅔ *cup split red lentils*
> *1⅓ cups water*
> *1 bay leaf*
> *1 cup grated Cheddar cheese*
> *1 medium-size onion, peeled and finely chopped*
> *½ cup button mushrooms, washed and finely chopped*
> *¼ cup fine fresh whole-grain bread crumbs*
> *1 tablespoon chopped parsley*
> *1 tablespoon lemon juice*
> *1 egg*
> *Sea salt*
> *Freshly ground black pepper*
> *2 teaspoons butter or margarine and 2 heaping tablespoons*
>   *dried bread crumbs for coating loaf pan*

Put the lentils, water, and bay leaf into a medium-size saucepan and simmer very gently, uncovered, until the lentils are tender and all the liquid has been absorbed, about 20 minutes. Remove the bay leaf. Preheat the oven to 375°F. Prepare a 1-pound loaf pan by putting a long narrow strip of wax paper on the base and up the sides. Grease the pan well with butter or margarine and sprinkle generously with dried crumbs. Add the cheese, onion, mushrooms, fresh bread crumbs, parsley, lemon juice, and egg to the lentils, mixing well. Season with plenty of salt and pepper. Spoon the mixture into the loaf pan and level the top. Bake, uncovered, for 45 to 60 minutes, or until firm and golden brown on top.

IF YOU DON'T EAT DAIRY PRODUCTS. Use grated Vegan Cheese (page 138) or crumbled tofu instead of the cheese, and

1 tablespoon soy flour blended to a smooth paste with water, instead of the egg. Season with yeast extract.

TO FREEZE. This loaf freezes well, and it's worth making a double batch if you like it. Cook, or half-cook the loaf, then freeze until firm and wrap in plastic. To use, unwrap and put the loaf back into a lightly greased tin. Bake in a moderate oven for about 40 minutes, or until heated through.

MIXED-NUT ROAST

Serves 4

> *Butter and dried bread crumbs (see page 55) for coating pan*
> *1 large onion, peeled and chopped*
> *3 tablespoons oil*
> *1 heaping tablespoon whole wheat flour*
> *¼ cup milk or water*
> *1 teaspoon yeast extract*
> *1 heaping teaspoon mixed dried herbs*
> *1½ cups whole wheat bread crumbs*
> *2 cups finely grated mixed nuts (use a selection of almonds, Brazil nuts, walnuts, roasted peanuts, hazelnuts, or cashews, as available)*
> *Sea salt*
> *Freshly ground black pepper*

Preheat the oven to 350°F. Grease a loaf pan with butter and line the base and short narrow sides with a piece of well-buttered wax paper; sprinkle with the dried bread crumbs.

Fry the onion in the oil for 10 minutes over moderate heat, browning lightly. Add the flour, stir for a minute, then pour in the milk or water and stir over the heat until very thick. Remove from the heat and add the rest of the ingredients. Season with salt and pepper to taste. Spoon the mixture into the prepared loaf pan, pressing down.

Bake for 45 minutes, or until it is firm in the center when touched lightly.

TO SERVE IMMEDIATELY. Slip a knife around the edge and turn the loaf out onto a warm serving dish. It's good with Vegetarian Gravy (page 140) and red-currant or cranberry jelly, or cold with Yogurt Dressing (page 109) and salad.

TO FREEZE. Bake for 20 minutes, let cool quickly, wrap and freeze. To serve, allow to thaw for 3 to 4 hours, then bake for 25 to 30 minutes.

RICE, CHEESE, AND SPINACH BAKE

Serves 4 to 6

> ¾ *cup raw brown rice*
> *1½ cups water*
> *Sea salt*
> *1 onion, peeled and chopped*
> *2 tablespoons oil*
> *16 ounces frozen spinach, thawed, or 2 pounds fresh spinach,*
> *cooked and drained*
> *½ pound grated sharp cheese*
> *Freshly ground black pepper*
> *¼ cup whole wheat bread crumbs and a little butter for topping*

Put the rice into a medium-size saucepan with the water and ½ teaspoon of the salt. Bring to a boil, cover, reduce the heat, and cook for 45 minutes. While the rice is cooking, fry the onion in the oil for 10 minutes over low heat, then add the spinach and remove from the heat. Add this mixture to the cooked rice, together with three-quarters of the cheese and salt and pepper to taste. Turn the mixture into a greased shallow ovenproof dish and sprinkle the bread crumbs and remaining grated cheese over the top. Dot with butter.

TO SERVE IMMEDIATELY. Bake for about 30 minutes at 400°F, or until the top is crisp.

IF YOU DON'T USE DAIRY PRODUCTS. Use grated Vegan Cheese (page 138).

TO FREEZE. Freeze before baking. To serve, allow to defrost for 5 to 6 hours, then bake as above.

SOY SAUSAGES

These sausages are far more nutritious than meat ones, since the soy and peanuts provide B vitamins, iron, calcium, and other valuable minerals. If you like this recipe, it would probably be worth making up a larger quantity: Use a 1-pound 2-ounce bag of soybeans, 1 pound peanuts, and multiply the rest of the ingredients by 5.

Serves 4

> 1 onion, peeled and finely chopped
> 2 tablespoons oil
> 1 clove garlic, peeled and crushed
> 1 cup cooked soybeans (see page 54)
> 1 cup grated roasted peanuts (see page 58)
> 1 tablespoon soy sauce
> 1 tablespoon tomato puree
> 1 tablespoon lemon juice
> 1 teaspoon mixed dried herbs
> Sea salt
> Freshly ground black pepper
> About 6 to 8 tablespoons whole wheat flour for coating
> Oil for shallow frying

Fry the onion in the oil for 10 minutes over moderate heat, browning lightly, then add the remaining ingredients, mashing everything together to make a paste. Form into sausage shapes and coat with whole wheat flour.

TO SERVE IMMEDIATELY. Shallow-fry in hot oil, turning the sausages so that they get crisp all over. Drain on paper towels.

TO FREEZE. Spread the sausages on a plate or baking sheet and freeze, uncovered, until solid. Transfer to a closed container. They can be used frozen as long as you fry them slowly to allow them to cook through. Or thaw for 1 to 2 hours, then fry in the usual way.

SOY AND WALNUT LOAF

Serves 4

> *2 teaspoons butter and 2 tablespoons dried bread crumbs (see*
>   *page 55) for coating pan*
> *1 onion, peeled and finely chopped*
> *2 stalks celery, finely chopped*
> *2 tablespoons oil*
> *1 cup cooked soybeans (see page 54)*
> *1 cup chopped walnuts*
> *2 tomatoes, skinned and chopped*
> *1 tablespoon tomato puree*
> *1 tablespoon lemon juice*
> *1 teaspoon mixed dried herbs*
> *2 eggs*
> *Sea salt*
> *Freshly ground black pepper*

Grease a loaf pan with butter and line the base and short narrow sides with a piece of well-buttered wax paper; sprinkle with the dried crumbs. Fry the onion and celery in the oil for 10 minutes over moderate heat, browning lightly. Remove from the heat and mix with the soybeans, walnuts, tomatoes, tomato puree, lemon juice, herbs, eggs, and salt and pepper to taste. Mix well, mashing the soybeans a bit to help bind the mixture together. Spoon into the prepared loaf pan, pressing down well.

TO SERVE IMMEDIATELY. Bake for 45 minutes at 350°F, or until firm in the center when touched lightly with your fingertips. Slip a knife around the edge and turn the loaf out onto a warm serving dish. It's good with Vegetarian Gravy (page 140) or Parsley Sauce (page 141) and cooked vegetables, or cold with pickles. It also makes a good filling for a soft whole wheat roll or pita bread.

IF YOU DON'T EAT DAIRY PRODUCTS. Replace the eggs with 2 tablespoons soy flour and 6 tablespoons water.

TO FREEZE. Bake as above but for only 20 minutes; let cool quickly, and freeze. To serve, allow to thaw for 3 to 4 hours, then bake at the same temperature for 25 to 30 minutes.

SPINACH QUICHE

This quiche is a useful and delicious way of eating your day's serving of dark green leafy vegetables!

Serves 4 as a main dish

¾ cup (packed) self-raising 85 percent flour
Pinch of salt
5 tablespoons butter or margarine, softened

FOR THE FILLING
One 10-ounce package of frozen spinach or 1 pound fresh spinach, washed, cooked, drained, and chopped
½ cup cottage or farmer cheese
1 egg
Sea salt
Freshly ground black pepper
Grated nutmeg
½ cup grated Cheddar cheese
2 tomatoes, sliced

Preheat the oven to 400°F. Put a baking sheet into the oven to heat up; standing the quiche on this helps the base to cook crisply. Grease an 8-inch quiche pan. Sift the flour and salt into a bowl. Add the butter or margarine and blend it in with your fingertips until the mixture looks like fine bread crumbs. Gently press the mixture together to make a dough; you won't need any water. Put the dough onto a lightly floured board, knead, then form into a smooth circle. Roll out thinly and lift gently into quiche pan. Press down; trim the edges. Prick the base, then bake for 15 minutes.

Meanwhile, mix together the spinach, cottage or farmer cheese, and egg. Season with salt, pepper, and grated nutmeg to taste. Spoon this mixture into the baked crust, sprinkle with the grated cheese, and arrange the tomatoes on top. Return the quiche to the oven, reduce the heat to 350°F, and bake for 30 minutes, or until it is puffed up and firm. Serve immediately, or let cool and freeze.

IF YOU DON'T EAT DAIRY PRODUCTS. Use 6 ounces soft tofu instead of the cottage cheese and egg. Use grated Vegan Cheese (page 138) instead of the dairy cheese.

TO FREEZE. Freeze the quiche, uncovered, until firm, then wrap. To serve, unwrap, thaw for 2 to 3 hours, then reheat in a moderate oven, to warm the quiche through.

VEGETABLE AND LIMA BEAN PIE

Serves 4–5

> 1 large onion, peeled and chopped
> 3 tablespoons oil
> 2 teaspoons unbleached flour
> 1 cup water
> 1 teaspoon yeast extract
> Sea salt
> Freshly ground black pepper
> 1 carrot, scraped and diced
> 1 stalk celery, chopped
> 1 leek, trimmed, cleaned, and sliced
> 2 tomatoes, peeled and chopped
> 1 cup sliced button mushrooms
> One 16-ounce can lima beans, or 1 cup home-cooked beans (see
>   page 54), drained
> 1½ cups whole wheat pastry made from 1½ cups (packed) 100
>   percent whole wheat flour, ¼ pound (1 stick) polyun-
>   saturated margarine, and 3 tablespoons cold water

Fry the onion in the oil for 10 minutes over low heat, then stir in the flour and allow to brown over the heat for 2 to 3 minutes. Pour in the water and add the yeast extract; stir until thickened. Season with salt and pepper to taste. Add the carrot, celery, and leek; cover, then simmer over gentle heat for about 15 minutes, or until the vegetables are cooked. Remove from the heat and add the tomatoes, mushrooms, and lima beans. Let cool while you make the pastry. Pour the vegetable mixture into a pie dish. Put an upturned egg cup in the center of the dish to support the pastry (it will get baked with the pie). Roll out the pastry rather thickly to fit the top of the dish. Cut ½-inch-wide strips from the trimmings; brush with cold water, place on the rim of pie dish, press down, brush with more cold water. Put the pastry on top of pie, trim.

TO SERVE IMMEDIATELY. Preheat the oven to 425°F. Make two steam holes in the pastry and bake for 20 minutes. Then reduce the heat to 400°F and bake for 20 minutes more.

TO FREEZE. This pie can be frozen before or after cooking. If freezing before cooking, don't make steam holes, because the liquid will expand and flow out. To serve, thaw for 6 to 8 hours, then make the steam holes if necessary. Bake the uncooked pie as described above; cover the cooked pie with foil and heat through in a moderate oven (350°F) for 20 to 30 minutes.

Quick Main Meals

However well stocked your deep freeze, you'll also need a repertoire of healthy dishes that need the minimum of preparation, for using before the baby is born when you're tired, and afterward, when you're tired and harried. It is quite true that on the whole it is more effort to make whole-food/vegetarian dishes than to put together a meal using convenience foods. But if you've stocked your shelves with the ingredients suggested on pages 54–58, you should find the following meals quick to make.

GRAIN DISHES, QUICHES, PASTA, AND PIZZA

BROCCOLI PILAF

Serves 4

> *1 onion, peeled and chopped*
> *1 tablespoon oil*
> *1 clove garlic, crushed*
> *1 tablespoon grated fresh ginger*
> *½ teaspoon turmeric*
> *1 cup raw long-grain brown rice*
> *2 cups water*
> *1 teaspoon salt*
> *¾ pound broccoli, washed, trimmed, and divided into small*
> *   florets*
> *1 red pepper, deseeded and diced*
> *Sea salt*
> *Freshly ground black pepper*
> *1 cup slivered almonds, toasted*

Gently fry the onion in the oil in a large saucepan for 5 minutes, then add the garlic, ginger, turmeric, and rice and cook, stirring, for 3 minutes. Add the water and salt. Increase the heat and bring to a boil, then cover, reduce heat, and cook very gently for 25 minutes. At this point put the broccoli and red pepper into the pan on top of the rice, but do not stir them into the rice. Put the lid back on the pan and cook very gently for a further 20 minutes, or until the vegetables and rice are tender and all the water has been absorbed. Stir gently with a fork and season as necessary with salt and pepper. Serve with the almonds sprinkled on top.

BROWN RICE WITH RED KIDNEY BEANS, TOMATOES, AND NUTS

Very quick and simple to make. Serve with a fresh watercress salad.

Serves 4

> *1 cup raw long-grain brown rice*
> *1 teaspoon sea salt*
> *½ teaspoon turmeric*
> *2 cups water*
> *1 tablespoon butter or margarine*
> *1 pound firm tomatoes, skinned and sliced*
> *1 cup cooked red kidney beans, drained, or one 16-ounce can, drained*
> *2 scallions, chopped*
> *1 cup walnut pieces or roasted peanuts*
> *Freshly ground black pepper*

Put the rice into a large saucepan with the salt, turmeric, and water. Bring to a boil, cover, reduce the heat, and cook for 45 minutes. Remove from the heat and allow the rice to stand for 10 to 15 minutes more. Put back over gentle heat. Add the butter or margarine, forking lightly through the rice; then add the tomatoes, beans, scallions, and walnuts or peanuts, turning the mixture gently with a fork until everything is evenly distributed and the tomatoes are heated through. Serve at once.

SPICED BROWN RICE WITH CURRY SAUCE

A pleasantly spicy mixture that's good with mango chutney and a salad made from sliced cucumber mixed with plain yogurt. Cuminseed is one of the traditional spices for stimulating the milk in breast-feeding mothers.

Serves 4

> 2 tablespoons oil
> ½ teaspoon turmeric
> 6 cloves
> 1 cup raw long-grain brown rice
> 2 cups water
> 1 teaspoon sea salt
>
> *FOR THE SAUCE*
> 1 onion, peeled and chopped
> 2 tablespoons oil
> 1 clove garlic, peeled and crushed
> 2 teaspoons cuminseed
> 2 teaspoons coriander
> 1 walnut-size piece of fresh ginger, peeled and grated
> 1½ cups canned tomatoes, with liquid
> Sea salt
> Freshly ground black pepper
> 4 hard-boiled eggs, peeled and sliced

Heat the oil in a medium-size saucepan. Add the turmeric and cloves and fry over medium heat for 1 to 2 minutes. Add the rice and stir for 2 to 3 minutes more. Add the water and salt. Bring to a boil, cover, reduce the heat, and cook very gently for 45 minutes.

Meanwhile make the sauce: Fry the onion gently in the oil without browning for 10 minutes; then add the garlic, cuminseed, and coriander. Stir for 1 to 2 minutes to cook the spices, then add the ginger and tomatoes. Mix well and add salt and pepper to taste. Stir gently. Cook over low heat for 15 minutes. Serve with the rice and hard-boiled egg slices. (This is too spicy for a baby.)

IF YOU DON'T EAT DAIRY PRODUCTS. Serve the curry with a side dish of roasted peanuts or pumpkin and sunflower seeds.

KASHA WITH MUSHROOMS, ONIONS, AND TOMATOES

Kasha is a natural remedy for varicose veins, high blood pressure, and hemorrhoids, so this is a good dish to try if you suffer from any of these. Apart from this, it tastes good and is quick to make. I like to serve it with sliced carrots in the winter, or zucchini in the summer, both sprinkled with parsley for extra iron and calcium.

Serves 4

> 2 cups water
> 1 teaspoon yeast extract
> 1 cup kasha
> Sea salt
> 1 large onion, peeled and chopped
> 3 tablespoons oil
> 2 cups button mushrooms, washed and sliced
> 1 cup chopped skinned tomatoes
> 1 cup cooked cannellini (white kidney beans), or one 16-ounce
>   can, drained
> Freshly ground black pepper

Put the water and yeast extract into a medium-size saucepan and bring to a boil. Add the kasha and a good pinch of salt. Cover, and cook over very gentle heat for 10 minutes, or until the water has been absorbed and the kasha is fluffy. Meanwhile, fry the onion in the oil for 7 minutes over gentle heat, then add the mushrooms, tomatoes, and beans. Cook, uncovered, for 3 minutes more. Season with salt and pepper to taste. Serve with the kasha.

BULGUR PILAF WITH RED PEPPERS AND LENTILS

Bulgur is wheat that has been cracked and steamed. It takes 15 minutes to prepare—as opposed to 45 minutes for brown rice—and is therefore especially useful for quick meals.

Serves 4

> *1 onion, peeled and chopped*
> *1 small red pepper, deseeded and chopped*
> *2 tablespoons oil*
> *1 clove garlic, peeled and crushed*
> *1 cup bulgur*
> *½ cup split red lentils*
> *3 cups boiling water*
> *1 teaspoon sea salt*
> *2 tablespoons chopped parsley*

Fry the onion and pepper in the oil for 10 minutes over gentle heat, then add the garlic and stir for a moment or two. Add the bulgur and heat, stirring, to brown it slightly. Then add the lentils, water, and salt. Bring to a boil, then reduce the heat, cover, and cook very gently for 30 minutes, or until the lentils and bulgur are tender and all the water has been absorbed. Correct the seasoning, fork the parsley through, and serve. This is nice with a tomato and onion salad, some watercress, and mango chutney.

BULGUR WITH PEACH AND RAISIN SAUCE

I like the sweetness of dried fruit with bulgur, especially the flavor of dried peaches.

Serves 4

> 1 cup bulgur
> 2 cups boiling water
> 1 teaspoon sea salt
> 1 tablespoon butter
> 1½ cups slivered almonds, toasted
>
> *FOR THE SAUCE*
> ¼ pound dried peaches (available from the health food store)
> 1¼ cups boiling water
> 1 onion, peeled and chopped
> 2 tablespoons oil
> 1 clove garlic, peeled and crushed
> 1 teaspoon cinnamon
> ¼ cup raisins

Put the bulgur into a large saucepan with the boiling water. Cover and let stand for 15 minutes.

Meanwhile make the sauce: Put the peaches into a bowl, cover with the boiling water, and set aside. Fry the onion in the oil over medium heat for 10 minutes, then add the garlic and cinnamon. In a blender or food processor, puree the peaches, together with their soaking water, and add to the onion mixture along with the raisins. Heat gently.

Heat the bulgur gently for 10 minutes, then drain off any remaining water and add the butter and almonds. Serve immediately, with the sauce.

BULGUR PILAF WITH RED PEPPERS, NUTS, AND RAISINS

The nuts, raisins, and cinnamon give this dish a Middle Eastern flavor. Serve with watercress or lettuce salad and some Yogurt Dressing (page 109), if you've time. You can reduce the cost of this recipe by using roasted peanuts (page 58) instead of the almonds.

Serves 4

> 1 cup bulgur
> 2 cups boiling water
> 1 teaspoon sea salt
> 1 onion, peeled and chopped
> 1 small red pepper, deseeded and chopped
> 2 tablespoons oil
> 1 teaspoon cinnamon
> ½ cup raisins
> 1½ cups slivered almonds

Put the wheat into a large bowl with the water and salt. Cover and allow to stand for 15 minutes. Meanwhile fry the onion and red pepper in the oil for 10 minutes over gentle heat, then add the cinnamon and stir for a moment or two. Drain the bulgur of any remaining water and add to the onion and pepper, together with the raisins and almonds. Stir gently over gentle heat for 5 to 10 minutes, or until heated through. Check seasoning and serve.

MILLET PILAF WITH MIXED VEGETABLES

Millet cooks in 20 minutes and has an attractive pale golden color and a pleasant flavor that makes a nice change from rice.

Serves 4

> *1 cup millet*
> *1 onion, peeled and chopped*
> *2 tablespoons oil*
> *2 cups water*
> *1 teaspoon sea salt*
> *1 cup frozen mixed vegetables*
> *1 cup cooked red kidney beans or one 16-ounce can, drained*
> *1 cup roasted peanuts (see page 58)*

First roast the millet by putting it into a dry saucepan and stirring it over moderate heat for 4 to 5 minutes, or until the millet begins to smell deliciously toasted, to be tinged with light brown, and some of the grains start to pop. Remove from the heat. Fry the onion in the oil in a medium-size saucepan for 10 minutes. Then add the millet, water, salt, mixed vegetables, and beans and bring to a boil. Cover, reduce the heat, and cook for 20 minutes, or until the millet is fluffy and all the water has been absorbed. Add the peanuts, fork through lightly, then serve. It's nice with some sliced tomatoes and watercress.

MILLET WITH ALMONDS AND TOMATO SAUCE

Serves 4

> *1 cup millet*
> *1 onion, peeled and chopped*
> *2 tablespoons oil*
> *2 cups water*

1 teaspoon sea salt
1 cup slivered almonds, toasted, or, for economy, use roasted
  peanuts (see page 58)

FOR THE SAUCE
1 onion, peeled and chopped
2 tablespoons oil
1½ cups canned tomatoes, with liquid
Sea salt
Freshly ground black pepper

Roast the millet as described in the previous recipe. Fry the onion in the oil in a medium-size saucepan over high heat for 10 minutes. Then add the millet, water, and salt and bring to a boil. Cover, reduce the heat, and cook for 20 minutes, or until the millet is fluffy and all the water has been absorbed.

Meanwhile make the sauce: Fry the onion in the oil for 10 minutes over gentle heat, or until soft, then add the tomatoes. Puree in a blender or food processor. Season to taste and return to the pan.

Add the almonds or peanuts to the millet, fork through lightly, then serve with the tomato sauce. Some watercress or lettuce in a light oil and vinegar dressing goes well with this.

CHEESE, TOMATO, AND ONION QUICHE

Time is saved in this recipe by not prebaking the quiche crust and by using easily prepared ingredients for the filling. The resulting quiche is light, and the pastry is tender and melts in your mouth.

Serves 4 as a main dish

> ¾ *cup self-raising 85 percent flour*
> *Sea salt*
> *5 tablespoons butter or margarine, softened*
>
> *FOR THE FILLING*
> ½ *cup grated Cheddar cheese, not packed*
> *6 scallions, chopped*
> *2 tomatoes, skinned and sliced*
> *Freshly ground black pepper*
> *1 egg*
> ½ *cup milk*

Preheat the oven to 375°F. Put a baking sheet into the oven to heat up; standing the quiche on this helps the base to cook crisply. Grease an 8-inch round quiche pan. Sift the flour and a pinch of the salt into a bowl. Add the butter or margarine and rub in with your fingertips until the mixture looks like fine bread crumbs. Gently press the mixture together to make a dough; you won't need any water. Put the dough onto a lightly floured board and knead; form into a smooth circle. Roll out thinly and lift gently into the prepared quiche pan. Press down; trim the edges; do not prick. Sprinkle the cheese and scallions over the pastry, then arrange the tomatoes on top and sprinkle with salt and pepper to taste. Whisk the egg and milk in a bowl with a little seasoning, then pour over the tomatoes. Bake the quiche for 40 minutes, or until the pastry is crisp and golden brown and the center is set and puffed up. Serve immediately, with a lettuce and cucumber salad or frozen peas and new potatoes.

IF YOU DON'T EAT DAIRY PRODUCTS. Make the filling as for the Mushroom and Tofu Quiche, using tomatoes instead of the mushrooms.

MUSHROOM AND TOFU QUICHE

The custard part of this quiche is made from tofu, yet it is almost identical to a light custard made from eggs and cream.

Serves 4 as a main dish

¾ cup self-raising 85 percent flour
Pinch of sea salt
5 tablespoons margarine, softened

FOR THE FILLING
1 onion, peeled and finely chopped
1 tablespoon margarine
1 clove garlic, peeled and crushed (optional)
1 cup white button mushrooms, washed and thinly sliced
10½ ounces soft tofu, mashed
Sea salt
Freshly ground black pepper
¼ cup ground almonds

Preheat the oven to 375°F. Put a baking sheet into the oven to heat up; standing the quiche on this helps the base to cook crisply. Grease an 8-inch round quiche pan.

Sift the flour and salt into a bowl. Rub in the margarine with your fingertips until the mixture looks like fine bread crumbs. Gently press together to make a dough; you won't need any water. Put dough onto a lightly floured board and knead; form into a smooth circle. Roll out thinly and lift gently into the prepared quiche pan. Press down; trim the edges; do not prick.

Fry the onion gently in the margarine for 7 minutes, then put in the garlic and mushrooms and cook for 3 minutes more. Remove from the heat, and stir in the mashed tofu. Season with salt and pepper to taste. Spoon into the pastry, level the top, and sprinkle with the almonds. Bake for 40 minutes, or until the pastry is crisp and golden brown and the center is set and puffed up. Serve immediately. This is good with new potatoes and a salad of watercress and lettuce, or frozen peas.

PASTA WITH LENTIL AND RED PEPPER SAUCE

A quickly made, iron-rich dish. I like it best with whole wheat pasta rings, rather than spaghetti.

Serves 4

> 1 onion, peeled and chopped
> 1 small red pepper, deseeded and chopped
> 2 tablespoons oil
> 1 clove garlic, peeled and crushed
> 1 teaspoon dried basil
> ¾ cup canned tomatoes, with liquid
> ½ cup split red lentils
> 1 tablespoon tomato puree
> 1½ cups water
> Sea salt
> Freshly ground black pepper
> Dash of sugar
> ½ pound whole wheat spaghetti or rings
> 1 tablespoon butter
> ½ cup grated Parmesan cheese to serve (optional)

Fry the onion and pepper in the oil in a large saucepan for 10 minutes over gentle heat, then add the garlic, basil, tomatoes, lentils, tomato puree, and water. Bring to a boil, reduce the heat, and leave to simmer gently, uncovered, for 15 to 20 minutes, or until the lentils are cooked. Season with salt and pepper to taste and the sugar.

About 15 minutes before the sauce is ready, start cooking the pasta. Half-fill a large saucepan with lightly salted water and bring to a boil.

Add the pasta, easing the spaghetti down into the water as the ends soften. Boil rapidly, uncovered, for about 10 minutes, or until a strand feels just tender when you bite it. Drain, then return to the pan with the butter and salt and pepper to taste. Serve with the sauce, handing around some grated cheese, if you're having this. Some watercress or a green salad is nice with it, too.

WHOLE WHEAT PASTA RINGS WITH TOMATO SAUCE

A beautifully quick dish. Serve with watercress or a watercress-based salad.

Serves 4

> *1 onion, peeled and chopped*
> *2 tablespoons oil*
> *1½ cups canned tomatoes, with liquid*
> *Sea salt*
> *Freshly ground black pepper*
> *¾ pound whole wheat pasta rings*
> *1 tablespoon butter*
> *Grated Parmesan cheese or Vegan Cheese (page 138) to serve*

Gently fry the onion in the oil in a medium-size saucepan for 10 minutes, or until softened, then add the tomatoes. Puree the mixture in a blender or food processor, return to the pan, season with salt and pepper to taste, and keep warm.

Meanwhile cook the pasta in a large saucepan half-filled with boiling salted water: It will take 8 to 10 minutes. Drain when the pasta is just tender, then return the pasta to the pan with the butter and salt and pepper to taste. Serve the pasta rings with the sauce, handing around the grated or vegan cheese.

SPAGHETTI WITH PESTO SAUCE

Pesto looks like a curious thick green mixture when it's first made, but when it's added to the hot, cooked spaghetti, it really transforms the pasta into something special with a delicious, rich flavor. You should really use fresh basil for this recipe, but if it's not easy to get, I find that a bunch of fresh parsley plus a good seasoning of dried basil makes a fairly good alternative.

Serves 4

> *FOR THE PASTA*
> *½ pound whole wheat spaghetti*
> *Sea salt*
> *2 tablespoons oil*
>
> *FOR THE PESTO*
> *2 cloves garlic, peeled and crushed*
> *1 large bunch fresh basil or a large bunch fresh parsley plus 2*
>   *to 3 teaspoons dried basil*
> *⅓ cup pine nuts*
> *⅓ cup grated Parmesan cheese*
> *½ cup olive oil*

Half-fill a large saucepan with water and add a teaspoon of the salt and the oil. Bring to a boil, then gently ease in the spaghetti, pushing it down into the water as it softens. Let the spaghetti simmer gently until it's just tender, about 10 minutes. Drain the spaghetti and return it to the hot saucepan.

While the spaghetti is cooking, make the pesto. Remove and discard the basil or parsley stalks and put the leaves into a blender or food processor together with the dried basil, if you're using it, the garlic, pine nuts, cheese, and oil. Blend at medium speed until you have a thick puree the consistency of softly whipped cream.

Put the pasta onto a hot serving dish and spoon the pesto on top; or serve the pesto separately and let everyone help themselves.

You'll perhaps want to serve a protein appetizer or dessert with this for a balanced meal, or you could offer a protein-rich salad.

QUICK PIZZA

Whole wheat pita bread makes an excellent base for a quick pizza. Serve with watercress or lettuce salad.

Serves 4

>*4 whole wheat pita breads*
>*1 cup cottage cheese*
>*8 tomatoes, skinned and sliced*
>*1 to 1½ cups sliced mozzarella cheese*
>*Sea salt*
>*Freshly ground black pepper*
>*Dried oregano*

Preheat the oven to 400°F or preheat the broiler. Put the pita bread on a baking sheet. Spread each with some cottage cheese, arrange the tomato slices on top, and scatter grated cheese over them. Sprinkle with salt, pepper, and oregano to taste. Bake for about 20 minutes or place under the broiler for about 10 minutes, or until the filling has heated through and the cheese has melted and browned.

IF YOU DON'T EAT DAIRY PRODUCTS. Use 10½ ounces of tofu (drained, mashed, and seasoned with salt and pepper) or Bean Spread (page 133), instead of the cottage cheese; and Vegan Cheese (page 138) for the topping.

BEAN AND LENTIL DISHES

QUICK CURRIED LIMA BEANS

More warming spices for breast-feeding moms. Serve with hot brown rice or, for extra iron, millet.

Serves 4

> *1 onion, peeled and chopped*
> *2 tablespoons oil*
> *1 clove garlic, peeled and crushed*
> *2 teaspoons cuminseed*
> *2 teaspoons coriander*
> *1 walnut-size piece fresh ginger, peeled and minced or grated*
> *Sea salt*
> *Freshly ground black pepper*
> *1 pound 4 ounces cooked lima beans, or two 16-ounce cans,*
>   *drained*
> *¾ cup water or cooking water drained from the lima beans (if*
>   *available)*

Fry the onion gently in the oil without browning for 10 minutes, then add the garlic, cuminseed, and coriander. Stir over the heat for 1 to 2 minutes to cook the spices, then add the ginger, beans, and water. Mix well and season with salt and pepper to taste. Cook over low heat for 15 minutes. (This is too spicy for a baby.) Serve over boiled brown rice, with mango chutney, lime pickle, sliced tomatoes, and onion rings on the side.

CREAMED CHICK-PEAS WITH CROUTONS

Very easy and delicious. Serve with some sliced tomatoes.

Serves 4

1 onion, peeled and chopped
2 tablespoons (preferably olive) oil
1 clove garlic, peeled and crushed
2 cups cooked chick-peas or two 15-ounce cans
¾ cup water or cooking water drained from the chick-peas (if
   available)
1 to 2 tablespoons lemon juice
Sea salt
Freshly ground black pepper

FOR THE CROUTONS
3 to 4 pieces whole wheat bread
Oil for shallow frying

Fry the onion gently in the oil without browning for 10 minutes, then add the garlic and chick-peas. Mash the chick-peas over the heat then add the water, beating with a wooden spoon to make a light mixture, like mashed potatoes. Add the lemon juice and salt and pepper to taste. Keep warm while you make the croutons.

Cut the crusts off the bread, then cut the bread into small dice. Fry in hot shallow fat until golden brown (about 2 to 3 minutes on each side), turning them so that they brown all over. Drain on paper towels. Serve the creamed chick-peas with the croutons.

VARIATION
The creamed chick-peas can be served with hot fingers of whole wheat toast if preferred.

CHILI RED BEANS

Another quick and easy bean dish that's good with some hot brown rice and a quickly made green salad. If you are making this for a baby, do not add the chili powder until the end, after you've taken out the baby's portion.

Serves 4

> *1 onion, peeled and chopped*
> *1 red pepper, deseeded and chopped*
> *2 tablespoons oil*
> *1½ cups canned tomatoes*
> *One 16-ounce can red kidney beans, or 1 cup home-cooked beans*
>   *(see page 54), drained*
> *1 teaspoon chili powder*
> *Sea salt*
> *Freshly ground black pepper*
> *Cooked brown rice, hot and ready to serve*

Fry the onion and red pepper gently in the oil without browning for 10 minutes, then add the tomatoes, red kidney beans, chili powder, and salt and pepper to taste. Stir over gentle heat for 5 to 10 minutes, or until the beans are heated through. Serve with the rice. If you're making this for a baby to share, remove the baby's portion before adding the chili powder and seasoning.

EASY CHEESE LENTILS

This is inexpensive and nourishing, rich in iron and calcium. Serve with sliced tomatoes and watercress.

Serves 4

> 1 onion, peeled and chopped
> 3 tablespoons oil
> 1 clove garlic, peeled and crushed
> 1 cup split red lentils
> 2½ cups water
> 1 cup grated Cheddar cheese
> Sea salt
> Freshly ground black pepper

Gently fry the onion in the oil for 10 minutes in a large saucepan. Add the garlic, lentils, and water. Bring to a boil, cover, reduce the heat, and cook gently for 15 to 20 minutes, or until the lentils are pale and soft. Beat in the grated cheese and season with salt and pepper. Serve at once.

IF YOU DON'T EAT DAIRY PRODUCTS. Use Vegan Cheese (page 138) instead of dairy cheese; season the lentils carefully —you may need to add a little yeast extract or miso and lemon juice.

SPICY LENTILS AND POTATOES

This is quick, easy, and inexpensive—and it's a good source of iron (which is found in both lentils and potatoes) and contains the warming spices that are helpful for breast-feeding. Serve with slices of firm raw tomato and some mango chutney. If a baby is going to share this with you, keep one section of the pan free from spices and avoid stirring this area. Serve the baby this portion first, then stir gently before serving the rest.

Serves 4

> 1 onion, peeled and chopped
> 3 tablespoons oil
> 1 clove garlic, peeled and crushed
> 1 teaspoon whole cuminseed
> 1 walnut-size piece of fresh ginger, peeled and finely grated
> 3 medium-size potatoes, peeled and cut into 1-inch cubes
> 1 cup split red lentils
> 2½ cups water
> Sea salt
> Freshly ground black pepper

Gently fry the onion in the oil for 10 minutes in a large saucepan or large, deep frying pan. Add the garlic, cuminseed, and ginger; stir-fry for 1 to 2 minutes. Then add the potatoes and stir for a further minute or two. Add the lentils, water, and a little seasoning; bring to a boil, cover, reduce the heat, and cook gently for 15 to 20 minutes, or until the lentils are pale and soft and the potatoes are just tender when pierced with a knife. Correct the seasoning and serve at once.

KHITCHARI

This is the dish from which the English kedgeree is derived. Although modern kedgeree is usually a fish dish, the original khitchari was a spicy mixture of rice and lentils, ideal for vegetarians.

The usual way of making this, and the method I used to use, is to cook the lentils and rice together. But it's difficult to judge the amount of water and the timing, and recently I've been cooking them separately, then mixing them together. I find that this gives a better result —light and slightly dry. I like khitchari with a juicy tomato salad and some mango chutney or lime pickle, but some people like to have curry sauce with it.

Serves 4

> ½ *pound split red lentils*
> 5 *cups water*
> 1 *bay leaf*
> 1 *cup raw brown rice*
> 2 *large onions*
> 2 *tablespoons butter*
> 1 *clove garlic, peeled and crushed*
> 2 *teaspoons curry powder*
> 1 *teaspoon cuminseed (optional)*
> *Sea salt and freshly ground black pepper*
> 1 *to* 2 *teaspoons lemon juice*

Put the lentils into a saucepan with 3 cups of the water and the bay leaf and simmer them gently until the lentils are tender and have absorbed most of the water, making a thickish puree. Remove the bay leaf. Keep the lentils warm.

While the lentils are cooking, boil the rice in the remaining 2 cups water for 40 to 45 minutes, or until just tender, then drain and rinse it.

Peel and chop the onions and sauté in the butter in a small saucepan over gentle heat for 5 minutes. Stir in the garlic, curry powder, and cuminseed and cook for 5 minutes more, or until the onion is softened but not browned.

To assemble the dish, gently mix together the rice and lentils—use a fork for this to avoid damaging the grains of rice—and gently stir in the onion mixture. Season with salt and pepper and add a little lemon juice to taste.

You can vary khitchari in a number of ways. It's good with sliced tomatoes, chopped hard-boiled eggs, or fried mushrooms or green pepper stirred in just before serving.

TOFU FRITTERS WITH LEMON

Meat eaters compare this to fried fish. It's delicious with the Yogurt Dressing (page 109) or Parsley Sauce (page 141) and a salad or quickly cooked vegetable. You need to allow time for the tofu to drain.

Serves 4

> *10 ounces firm tofu*
> *Sea salt*
> *Freshly ground black pepper*
> *Lemon juice*
> *About ½ cup whole wheat flour*
> *Oil for shallow frying*
> *Lemon wedges*

Drain the tofu in a colander, being careful not to break it up. Cut it into ¼-inch slices, sprinkle each with salt, pepper, and a few drops of lemon juice, and coat in flour. Shallow-fry in oil over moderate heat about 3 minutes on each side, or until crisp and golden brown on both sides. Drain on paper towels. Serve at once, with the lemon wedges.

MAIN-COURSE VEGETABLE AND NUT DISHES

Several of these vegetable dishes are good with a crunchy savory seed mix sprinkled over them. To make this, mix 2 heaping tablespoons sesame seeds and 2 heaping tablespoons pumpkin or sunflower seeds or roasted peanuts with 2 tablespoons soy sauce. Make sure that all the seeds or nuts are coated with soy sauce. Spread the mixture out on an ungreased baking sheet and bake at 400°F for 10 to 15 minutes. Let cool; the mixture will get crisp as it cools. You can of course make this up in a larger quantity if you like it.

QUICK ALMOND AND MUSHROOM NUTMEAT

Serve this with new potatoes and a cooked green vegetable or use it as a filling for parboiled green peppers, then bake. It's also good as a filling for a baked whole wheat quiche crust. This dish contains iron —in the almonds, bread, and parsley—as well as B vitamins from these and from the mushrooms.

Serves 4

> *½ cup boiling water*
> *1 teaspoon yeast extract*
> *4 slices whole wheat bread, crusts removed*
> *1 onion, peeled and finely chopped*
> *2 tablespoons oil*
> *2½ cups button mushrooms, washed and sliced*
> *1 cup almonds, ground*
> *1 tablespoon soy sauce*
> *1 tablespoon lemon juice*
> *Sea salt*
> *Freshly ground black pepper*
> *Chopped parsley and lemon wedges to serve*

Put the boiling water, yeast extract, and bread into a bowl; set aside. Fry the onion in the oil over gentle heat, for 7 minutes, browning slightly, then add the mushrooms and fry for 3 minutes more. Stir in the bread and water mixture, the almonds, soy sauce, lemon juice, and salt and pepper to taste, adding a little extra water if necessary to give a soft consistency. Mix gently, cook for a few minutes more to heat everything through, then serve, sprinkled with chopped parsley and garnished with lemon wedges. Some fingers of hot whole wheat toast are pleasant with this, if you want a crisp texture for contrast.

EASY CAULIFLOWER CHEESE

Serves 4

> *1 large cauliflower*
> *Sea salt*
> *2 cups grated cheese*

Preheat the broiler to moderately hot. Wash and trim the cauliflower, dividing it into small florets as you do so. Heat 1 inch salted water in a saucepan and cook the cauliflower for about 4 minutes, or until just tender. Drain well and place in a lightly greased shallow ovenproof dish. Cover with the grated cheese and place under the grill until the cheese has melted and is beginning to brown. Serve immediately, with hot whole wheat toast or rolls and a salad of watercress or sliced tomatoes.

IF YOU DON'T EAT DAIRY PRODUCTS. Use Vegan Cheese (page 138) instead of dairy cheese.

CAULIFLOWER WITH PEANUT AND TOMATO SAUCE

This is suitable for a baby to share as long as you grind up the peanuts finely.

Serves 4

FOR THE SAUCE
1 onion, peeled and chopped
2 tablespoons oil
1 tablespoon peanut butter
1 cup roasted peanuts (see page 58), chopped or ground
1 pound tomatoes, skinned and chopped, or one 15-ounce can
Sea salt
Freshly ground black pepper
1 large cauliflower

Start by making the sauce: Fry the onion in the oil over gentle heat for 10 minutes, then add the peanut butter, peanuts, and tomatoes. Season with salt and pepper to taste and keep warm. Wash and trim the cauliflower, dividing it into small florets as you do so. Heat 1 inch salted water in a saucepan and cook the cauliflower for about 5 minutes, or until tender. Serve the cauliflower with the sauce spooned over it.

QUICK NUT RISSOLES

Another recipe containing buckwheat (another name for kasha is buckwheat groats), with its valuable rutin (see page 146), as well as iron from the almonds and parsley.

Serves 4

> 1 onion, peeled and finely chopped
> 4 tablespoons (½ stick) margarine
> 1 cup buckwheat flour
> 1¼ cups water
> 1 teaspoon yeast extract
> 1 cup almonds, ground
> 2 heaping tablespoons chopped parsley
> Sea salt
> Freshly ground black pepper
> ¼ to ½ cup whole wheat flour, oatmeal, or bread crumbs to coat
> Oil for shallow frying

Fry the onion in the margarine over moderate heat for 10 minutes. Stir in the buckwheat flour, then the water, to make a thick sauce. Cook for 3 to 4 minutes, then remove from the heat and add the rest of the ingredients, seasoning with salt and pepper to taste. If there's time, let the mixture cool. Form into rissoles, making them round and flat like burgers, and coat in flour, oatmeal, or bread crumbs, and shallow-fry, turning the rissoles to cook both sides. Serve with a green salad, or with chutney in a soft whole wheat roll, or with Vegetarian Gravy (page 140) and cooked vegetables (carrots and mashed potatoes go particularly well with these).

BAKED POTATOES WITH VARIOUS TOPPINGS

One of the great convenience foods, a baked potato makes an excellent simple main course. Grated cheese is probably the most popular topping, but cottage cheese or sour cream and chopped chives are also good. If you don't eat dairy products or if you want a change, tofu mashed with chopped chives or scallions, grated hard soy cheese, or one of the bean or nut spreads on pages 133 and 136–37 are also good. One of my daughters likes her potato best with homemade Tomato Sauce (page 142).

Serves 4

> *4 medium-large potatoes (about ½ pound each)*
> *Oil (optional)*
> *Topping as desired (see recipe headnote)*

Preheat the oven to 450°F. Scrub the potatoes, then prick them in several places to allow steam to escape. Rub them lightly with oil if you like, then place them in a baking pan and bake for 1 to 1½ hours, or until the potatoes feel soft when squeezed lightly in the center. Serve with the selected topping or with a salad—they're particularly good with Cabbage, Apple, and Raisin Salad (page 117).

POTATO CAKES WITH NUTS OR SUNFLOWER SEEDS

These are especially quick if you plan for them in advance and cook extra potatoes the previous day. They're nice with the Cabbage, Apple, and Raisin Salad (page 117), or with a simple salad of lettuce and sliced tomatoes.

Serves 4

> *1 pound potatoes*
> *2 tablespoons butter or margarine*
> *Milk or soy milk*
> *1 cup almonds, cashew, or sunflower seeds, finely ground*
> *2 tablespoons chopped scallions*
> *Sea salt*
> *Freshly ground black pepper*
> *About ¼ to ½ cup whole wheat flour for coating*
> *Oil for shallow frying*

Scrub or peel the potatoes and cut into even-size pieces, about 1 inch square. Cover with water and boil gently until tender (about 15 to 20 minutes), then drain and mash. (You can mash them with the skins on for extra fiber and nourishment if you like.) Beat in the butter or margarine and enough milk to make a creamy consistency, then add the nuts or sunflower seeds and the scallions. Stir in a little more milk if necessary to make a soft consistency that holds together. Season with salt and pepper to taste. Divide into 8 burger-shaped pieces, form into "cakes," and coat in whole wheat flour. Fry quickly in a little hot oil (in two batches if necessary); drain on kitchen towels. Serve immediately.

MAIN-COURSE MASHED POTATOES

One of my emergency standbys when I was hard-pressed with two babies under two years old. I would serve this with watercress or frozen peas.

Serves 4

> 2¼ pound potatoes, peeled and cut into 1-inch cubes
> 1 tablespoon butter or margarine
> ¾ cup milk or soy milk
> 1½ cups grated Cheddar cheese
> Sea salt
> Freshly ground black pepper
> 2 tomatoes, sliced

Boil the potatoes in water to cover for 15 to 20 minutes, or until tender, drain, and mash with the butter and milk. Preheat the broiler. Beat in most of the grated cheese and season with salt and pepper to taste. Spread the mixture in a broiler pan or suitable ovenproof dish. Put the tomato slices on top and sprinkle with the rest of the cheese. Broil for 5 to 10 minutes, or until the top is golden brown. Serve immediately.

IF YOU DON'T EAT DAIRY PRODUCTS. You could use Vegan Cheese (page 138) instead of dairy cheese, but a better variation, I think, is to mix a heaping tablespoon each of sesame seeds and sunflower seeds with a tablespoon of soy sauce and sprinkle this all over the top before broiling. Don't place the dish too near the heat, because the sesame seeds catch easily.

EASY RATATOUILLE

Ratatouille is economical if you make it when zucchini are in season, and it can be served as a main dish, with cooked rice, millet, bulgur, kasha, or potatoes, with grated cheese or toasted pumpkin and sunflower seeds to accompany it.

Serves 4

> *2 large onions, peeled and chopped*
> *2 tablespoons oil*
> *1 large clove garlic, peeled and crushed*
> *2 red peppers, deseeded and chopped*
> *1 pound zucchini, washed and sliced*
> *1½ cups canned tomatoes, with liquid*
> *Sea salt*
> *Freshly ground black pepper*
> *Chopped parsley to serve (optional)*

Fry the onions gently in the oil in a large saucepan for 10 minutes without browning. Add the garlic, red peppers, and zucchini and fry for 5 minutes more, stirring often. Then stir in the tomatoes and salt and pepper to taste. Cook gently for 15 minutes, or until the vegetables are tender. Correct the seasoning and serve, sprinkled with lots of chopped parsley if available. Alternatively, fork plenty of chopped parsley into the brown rice or other grains to give them a pretty green color and add to the nourishment of the dish.

STIR-FRIED VEGETABLES

These are quick to do as long as you choose vegetables that do not need much preparation. I like to use broccoli because it is such an attractive color and one of the most nutritious vegetables of all. Use home-grown bean sprouts (pages 111–12), if you have them.

Serves 4

>*2 tablespoons oil*
>*1½ pounds broccoli, washed, trimmed, and cut into small pieces*
>*1 small red pepper, deseeded and finely chopped*
>*3 cups bean sprouts*
>*1 bunch scallions, trimmed and chopped*
>*1 walnut-size piece of fresh ginger, peeled and finely grated*
>*Sea salt*
>*Freshly ground black pepper*
>*1 cup almonds, roasted peanuts, or pumpkin seeds*

Just before you want to eat, heat the oil in a wok or large saucepan. Put in all the vegetables and the ginger and stir-fry for 1 to 2 minutes, or until they're heated through. Season with salt and pepper to taste; stir in the nuts or seeds. Serve with hot brown rice, millet, bulgur, or warm pita bread. (If you're serving it with a grain, remember to get it cooked before you start stir-frying!)

VEGETABLE STEW

Although eggplant isn't usually the least expensive of vegetables, this stew can make quite an economical main course if you serve it with some grated cheese or roasted nuts and seeds and a cooked grain, such as millet or bulgur.

Serves 4

> *1 large eggplant*
> *Sea salt*
> *1 large onion, peeled and chopped*
> *3 tablespoons oil*
> *2 cloves garlic, peeled and crushed*
> *1½ cups canned tomatoes, with liquid*
> *Sea salt*
> *Freshly ground black pepper*
> *2 stalks celery, sliced*
> *12 ounces carrots, scraped and sliced*
> *½ cup button mushrooms, washed and sliced*
> *Chopped parsley*
> *Grated hard cheese*

Trim the eggplant and cut it into ½-inch dice. Place this in a colander, sprinkle with salt, place a plate and a weight on top, and leave for about 30 minutes. Then rinse under cold water and squeeze as dry as possible in your hands.

Fry the onion in 1 tablespoon of the oil over gentle heat for 10 minutes. Add the garlic and tomatoes, liquidize in a blender, and season with salt and pepper to taste.

Heat the remaining 2 tablespoons oil in a large saucepan and fry the eggplant, celery, carrots, and mushrooms for 10 minutes. Add the tomato mixture. Cook over gentle heat for 20 minutes, or until the vegetables are tender. Serve with hot cooked brown rice and hand around grated cheese separately if you like.

SPICED VEGETABLES WITH DHAL SAUCE

This is a lovely dish, not hot but lightly spiced. The dhal sauce supplies the protein, and it's nice served with hot cooked brown rice, pappadums, mango chutney, and the Chinese Cabbage, Tomato, and Scallion Salad on page 122.

Serves 4

> 3 tablespoons oil
> 1 onion, peeled and chopped
> 1 large clove garlic, peeled and crushed
> 1 teaspoon turmeric
> 1 teaspoon coriander
> 1 teaspoon cumin
> 1 bay leaf
> 2 carrots, about ½ pound, scraped and thinly sliced
> 1 pound potatoes, peeled and cubed
> 2 leeks, washed and sliced
> ⅔ cup water
> Sea salt
> Freshly ground black pepper

> *FOR THE DHAL SAUCE*
> 1 onion, peeled and chopped
> 1 clove garlic, peeled and crushed
> 1 tablespoon oil
> ⅔ cup split red lentils
> 1 teaspoon coriander
> 1 teaspoon cumin
> 2½ cups vegetable stock or water
> 1 bay leaf

Heat the oil in a fairly large saucepan and sauté the onion over moderate heat for 5 minutes, then add the garlic, spices, and bay leaf and stir over the heat for 1 to 2 minutes. Add the remaining vegetables and stir over the heat for 1 to 2 minutes more so that they are all coated with the oil and spices. Add the water and salt and pepper to taste. Cover and simmer for 15 to 20 minutes, or until the vegetables are all tender, stirring from time to time and checking to make sure they do not cook dry—there will be very little water left. Alternatively, the spiced vegetables can be put into an ovenproof casserole and baked at 325°F for about 1 to 1½ hours, or until tender when pierced with the point of a knife.

To make the sauce, first sauté the onion and garlic in the oil over moderate heat for 5 minutes, or until softened; then stir in the lentils and spices and cook for a minute or two more. Add the stock or water and the bay leaf; bring to a boil, then simmer gently for 15 to 20 minutes, or until the lentils are tender and pale gold in color. Remove the bay leaf, puree the sauce, and add salt and pepper to taste.

Serve the vegetables with the sauce.

RED CABBAGE AND CHESTNUT CASSEROLE

Real warming winter food this, a rich burgundy-colored casserole of succulent red cabbage and sweet-tasting chestnuts cooked with butter, onions, and red wine. It's lovely as a main dish for the adult members of the family; serve it with baked potatoes that have been split and filled with sour cream and chopped chives. Leftovers are very good as a cold salad. I rather lazily tend to use dried chestnuts but you could use fresh ones. You'll need about a pound for this recipe. Add them to the casserole with the wine and seasoning.

Serves 3 to 4

> ¼ *pound dried chestnuts*
> 1 *large onion*
> 4 *tablespoons (½ stick) butter*
> 1½ *pounds red cabbage*
> ⅔ *cup dry red wine*
> *Sea salt*
> *Freshly ground black pepper*
> *Sugar*

Cover the chestnuts with plenty of cold water and leave them to soak for several hours. Cook them gently, covered, until they're tender; this will take 1 to 1½ hours and you'll need to watch the level of the water and probably add some more so that they don't cook dry. Drain the chestnuts.

Preheat the oven to 300°F. Peel and chop the onion and sauté in the butter for 10 minutes over gentle heat. Meanwhile, shred the cabbage, add this to the onion, and turn the mixture so that everything is coated with the butter. Stir in the chestnuts, wine, and salt and pepper to taste. Bring to a boil, transfer to an ovenproof casserole, cover, and bake for 2 to 3 hours, until the cabbage is very tender. Correct the seasoning—you'll probably need to add more salt and pepper and some sugar to bring out the flavor.

This dish can be made in advance and reheated—in fact, I think this actually improves the flavor—and it can also be cooked at the bottom of a hotter oven if you want to bake potatoes at the same time.

ASPARAGUS CASSEROLE

This savory pudding is called a *sformato* in Italy and is a cross between a soufflé and a loaf. I think it's best served straight from the dish with something crisp—hot garlic bread if you're serving it as a first course, toasted triangles of bread or crunchy golden roast potatoes and a good tomato sauce on the side for a main course.

Serves 4 as a main dish, 6 as a first course

> *3 tablespoons butter*
> *3 tablespoons all-purpose flour*
> *1¼ cups milk*
> *2 to 3 tablespoons grated Parmesan cheese*
> *Sea salt*
> *Freshly ground black pepper*
> *3 eggs*
> *1 pound asparagus spears, steamed and cut into 1-inch pieces*
> *1 tablespoon chopped fresh parsley*
> *Triangles of toasted bread*

Preheat the oven to 350°F. In a heavy-bottomed saucepan melt the butter and stir in the flour. When it's blended, add the milk in three batches; keep the heat fairly high and stir constantly each time, until the mixture thickens, before adding any more. Take the saucepan off the heat and add the grated cheese and salt and pepper to taste.

Beat the eggs and drain the asparagus. Mix the eggs into the sauce and then gently stir in the asparagus and parsley. Correct the seasoning, then pour the mixture into a lightly buttered shallow ovenproof dish. Put the dish into another dish or pan containing about 1 inch of very hot water and place it on the center rack of the oven. Bake for about 1 hour, or until the mixture is set. Serve with triangles of toasted bread.

HOT AVOCADO WITH WINE STUFFING

This avocado dish makes a delicious, luxurious main course for the adult members of the family. Make sure that the avocados are really ripe—they should just yield to fingertip pressure all over. It's important to leave the preparation of the avocados until the last minute and only just warm them through in the oven, though the filling can be made in advance.

Serves 6

1 cup finely grated Brazil nuts
1 cup grated Swiss cheese
1 cup soft whole wheat bread crumbs
One 8-ounce can tomatoes
1 small garlic clove, peeled and crushed
1 tablespoon tomato paste
2 tablespoon chopped fresh chives
4 to 6 tablespoons dry sherry
Sea salt
Freshly ground black pepper
Tabasco sauce
3 ripe avocados
Juice of 1 lemon
A little extra grated cheese and bread crumbs for topping

First make the stuffing: Put the nuts, cheese, bread crumbs, tomatoes, garlic, tomato paste, and chives into a bowl and mix together. Stir in enough sherry to make a soft mixture that will just hold its shape, then season with salt to taste, plenty of pepper, and enough Tabasco sauce to give the mixture a pleasant tang. Set aside until just before the meal —you can make the stuffing a few hours ahead if convenient.

Preheat the oven to 450°F. Just before the meal, halve the avocados and remove the skin and pits. Mix the lemon juice with a good pinch of salt and a grinding of pepper and brush all over the avocados. Place the avocados in a shallow ovenproof dish. Spoon the stuffing mixture into them, dividing it evenly among them; sprinkle a little cheese and a few bread crumbs on top of each. Put the avocados into the oven and reduce the heat to 400°F. Bake for 15 minutes. Serve immediately. (I find it best to put the avocados into the oven just as everyone sits down for their first course—it's important that they not be overcooked.) They are delicious with creamy mashed potatoes and a lightly cooked vegetable, such as baby carrots.

Desserts

From the point of view of health, fresh fruit is perhaps the best dessert there is. If you think that fresh fruit is expensive, it's worth checking the price of fruit in season with that of another sweet. It usually compares favorably. However, I know many families don't feel they've had a meal unless they finish with a dessert, so here are some ideas for ones that are quick and nutritious.

First of all, here are three useful toppings that taste good and are much better for you than cream, and a crunchy garnish that is a good way of adding some nutritious sesame seeds to a dessert.

CREAMY TOFU AND ALMOND TOPPING

This works out at about the same price as a 6-ounce carton of heavy cream, but unlike cream, it contains useful amounts of iron, calcium, and other minerals.

Serves 4

> 1 cup soft tofu
> ¼ cup ground almonds
> 1 teaspoon honey
> ½ to 1 teaspoon vanilla extract (real vanilla extract from the
>   health food store, if possible)

Drain excess water from the tofu, then put the tofu into a bowl with the other ingredients and beat until creamy.

WHIPPED TOFU TOPPING

This one works out to be even less expensive than a small carton of heavy cream. It has a lovely whipped texture and it is, at the same time, nutritious.

Serves 4

> 1 cup tofu
> 2 tablespoons unsalted margarine
> ¼ cup turbinado sugar or honey
> ½ to 1 teaspoon vanilla extract (real vanilla extract from the
>   health food store if possible)

Drain the tofu in a sieve, then blot it dry with a soft cloth. Beat the margarine and sugar or honey until light and fluffy, then gradually add the tofu, a little at a time, beating well between each addition, to make a light, fluffy mixture. Flavor with vanilla.

CASHEW OR ALMOND CREAM

A pleasant, pouring cream that is delicious over fruit salads and dried-fruit compotes like the one on pages 210–11. It works out at about the same price as a large carton of light cream. You need a blender or food processor to make this one.

Makes 1¼ to 1½ cups

> 1 cup cashew pieces
> ½ cup water
> 1 to 2 teaspoons turbinado sugar or honey

Put all the ingredients into a blender or food processor and whizz to a cream. It can be thinned with the addition of a little more water if you like.

CRUNCHY SESAME TOPPING

This is marvelous sprinkled over plain yogurt or a creamy pudding like the Apricot Fool on page 208 and keeps well in an airtight jar. Sesame seeds are rich in calcium.

> *1 teaspoon butter or margarine*
> *¼ cup (packed) brown sugar (make sure it's the real thing, from*
> *the health food store)*
> *⅛ cup sesame seeds*

Put the butter or margarine and sugar into a small saucepan and heat gently, or until the sugar has melted, lost its granular appearance, and is bubbling at the edges; this only takes a couple of minutes or so. Remove from the heat, stir in the sesame seeds, and turn the mixture out onto a piece of wax paper. Spread it out with a knife or the palm of your hand so that it is about ¼ inch thick. Let cool, then crush into little chunky pieces with a rolling pin.

BAKED APPLES WITH RAISINS

Easy, nutritious, and delicious served with Creamy Tofu and Almond Topping (page 203), Cashew or Almond Cream (page 204), or some chilled plain yogurt.

Serves 4

> *4 medium-size cooking apples*
> *½ cup raisins*

Preheat the oven to 400°F. Wash the apples and remove cores, then score around the center of each with a sharp knife, just piercing the skin to prevent them from bursting as they cook. Place the apples in an ovenproof dish. Fill the centers with the raisins. Bake for 45 minutes, or until the apples are tender.

APPLES WITH RAISINS

In this recipe, the raisins add extra food value (iron and B vitamins) as well as sweetness, so that little or no extra sweetening is needed. If this is sieved or pureed after cooking, it's excellent for a baby.

Serves 4

> *2 pounds apples*
> *2 tablespoons butter or margarine*
> *1 cup raisins*
> *Honey to taste*

Peel, core, and slice the apples. Melt the butter or margarine in a heavy-bottomed saucepan and add the apples and raisins. Stir, cover, and cook gently for about 10 minutes, or until the apples are soft. Stir the mixture from time to time as it cooks to avoid burning. This is good either hot or cold.

VARIATION
This is equally good made with dates instead of raisins. Use cooking dates and check them to make sure there are no pits.

TO FREEZE. Let cool quickly, spoon into a suitable covered container, and freeze. To serve, allow to thaw for several hours at room temperature.

APRICOTS WITH CASHEW CREAM

This is a particularly nutritious dessert, being especially rich in vitamin A, calcium, and iron and a pleasant mixture of flavors and textures. It's best to soak the apricots overnight if possible. Puree them if serving to a baby.

Serves 4

> 1 pound dried apricots
> 1 cup cashews
> 1 to 2 teaspoons honey
> ½ teaspoon vanilla extract
> ¾ cup water

Wash the apricots well in warm water, then put them into a bowl and let soak in cold water to cover for several hours. If they seem soft enough to eat as they are, drain, reserving the water, and put them in serving dishes. If they still seem rather firm, put them into a saucepan with their soaking water and simmer gently, uncovered, for 20 to 30 minutes, or until the apricots are tender and the water has become syrupy. Let cool, then put into serving dishes as before.

To make the topping, put the cashews into a blender or food processor along with the honey, vanilla, and water (if you drained the apricots, use this water). Blend until creamy-looking and fairly smooth, adding a little more water if necessary to make the consistency you want. Pour over the apricots and serve.

TO FREEZE. The prepared apricots and the topping can be frozen separately in suitable containers. To serve, remove from freezer and leave to stand at room temperature for 2 to 3 hours, or until thawed. Stir the topping before use.

APRICOT FOOL

This is not an inexpensive dessert, but it is easy to make and rich in both iron and calcium. An excellent dessert for a baby.

Serves 4 to 6

> 3 cups dried apricots
> 1½ cups soft white low-fat cheese, such as farmer cheese, or ½
>   pound firm tofu
> 2 tablespoons honey
> Crunchy Sesame Topping (page 205) to garnish (optional)

Wash the apricots well in warm water, then soak them in cold water to cover for several hours. If they still seem rather firm, cook them gently in their soaking liquid until tender (20 to 30 minutes); let cool. Drain the apricots, then put them into a blender or food processor with the cheese or tofu and the honey and blend until smooth. Spoon into individual bowls, sprinkling with the sesame topping just before serving if you wish.

TO FREEZE. Spoon the mixture into a suitable container and freeze. To serve, thaw at room temperature for several hours.

BANANA WITH CAROB SAUCE

This is a popular and nutritious dessert for children.

Serves 4

> 2 tablespoons brown sugar
> 2 tablespoons carob powder
> ½ cup water
> ½ cup evaporated milk or concentrated soy milk

3 to 4 bananas
2 tablespoons slivered almonds

Put the sugar and carob powder into a saucepan and gradually stir in the water. Bring to a boil, then simmer for about 10 minutes, or until the mixture is thick and syrupy. Remove from heat and stir in the evaporated milk or concentrated soy milk. Peel and slice the bananas, dividing them among 4 bowls. Pour the carob sauce over the bananas and sprinkle with the almonds.

BANANA CUSTARD

Another dessert that children love, and a good way of getting milk into reluctant milk drinkers! Gelose is a vegetarian gelatin made from seaweed. It comes in the form of a powder and can be bought from the health food store.

Serves 4

2 teaspoons gelose
2 cups milk
1 to 2 tablespoons honey
A few drops of real almond extract
A few drops of real vanilla extract
3 to 4 bananas
A little grated carob bar or slivered almonds to garnish

Put the gelose in a saucepan with a little of the milk and blend until smooth; add the rest of the milk and the honey, and bring to a boil over gentle heat; simmer for 2 minutes. Flavor with a few drops of almond and vanilla extracts. Peel and slice the bananas, dividing them among 4 dishes. Strain the gelose mixture over the bananas. Leave to set about 60 minutes. Top with a little grated carob bar or a few slivered almonds before serving if you wish.

CAROB (OR CHOCOLATE) PUDDING

This is another dessert that children usually seem to like, and, again, it's a useful way of giving them milk. My children like the chocolate version best, and chocolate is a useful source of iron and other minerals.

Serves 4 to 6

> *1 tablespoon carob or cocoa powder*
> *3 tablespoons turbinado sugar*
> *2 teaspoons gelose*
> *1 teaspoon real vanilla extract*
> *2 cups milk*
> *A little grated carob or chocolate bar to garnish*

Put the carob or cocoa powder into a saucepan with the sugar, gelose, and vanilla. Mix to a smooth paste with a little of the milk, then gradually add the rest. Heat this mixture to boiling, stirring all the time, then simmer for 2 minutes, continuing to stir. Pour the mixture into 4 or 6 individual dishes; let cool, then chill. Top with a little grated carob or chocolate before serving.

DRIED-FRUIT COMPOTE

This is packed with iron and other minerals. It's good on its own or with plain yogurt or Cashew or Almond Cream (page 204). Puree or sieve if serving to a baby.

Serves 4 to 6

> *1½ cups mixed dried fruit*
> *Boiling water*

Wash the dried fruit well in warm water, then put it into a bowl, cover generously with boiling water, and leave to soak for several hours. Then put the fruit into a saucepan, together with the water in which it was soaked, and simmer gently, uncovered for 20 to 30 minutes, or until the fruit is tender and the water syrupy and much reduced. Let cool, then chill.

TO FREEZE. Spoon the fruit into a suitable container, leaving room for expansion, and freeze. To serve, remove from the freezer and let stand at room temperature for several hours, or until thawed.

FIGS WITH YOGURT AND SESAME SEEDS

This dessert supplies over half the recommended daily calcium allowance during pregnancy, so if you, like me, are fond of these particular ingredients, it's a useful dessert (or breakfast) dish.

Serves 1

> *¼ pound dried figs, chopped*
> *¾ cup plain yogurt*
> *1 rounded tablespoon sesame seeds*

Put the figs into a bowl, pour the yogurt over them, and sprinkle with the sesame seeds.

FRUIT SALAD

Any fruit in season can be used for this, and because of their high nutritional value, I often slip in a few dried fruits, too, as in this recipe.

Serves 4

> *¼ pound dried whole apricots*
> *8 to 10 small prunes*
> *Boiling water*
> *2 large juicy oranges*
> *1 large eating apple, with a rosy skin if possible, washed*
> *1 banana*

Put the dried apricots and prunes into a bowl and cover with boiling water. Let soak for several hours, then stew them gently in a saucepan, with their soaking water, for about 20 minutes if necessary, to make them more tender. Let cool and put the fruit along with its soaking water into a bowl. Hold the oranges over the bowl (to catch the juice) and cut off the skin, going around and around as if you were peeling an apple. Then cut the segments of flesh away from the skin and membranes and add these to the bowl. Slice the apple; peel and slice the banana; and add these to the bowl. Spoon into individual serving dishes. This is good on its own, or with one of the toppings on pages 203–5.

KIDS' FAVORITE ICE CREAM

This ice cream is always popular with children; I have never been quite sure why, to be honest, but as it's an excellent way of getting them to eat milk, I don't argue with them! My children prefer the chocolate version, but you can also make it with carob if you prefer. This recipe also makes delicious ice pops if you freeze it in little individual molds.

Serves 6

> 1 tablespoon corn meal or arrowroot
> 1½ tablespoons sugar
> 3 cups milk
> ¼ pound plain chocolate or carob bar
> 1 cup evaporated milk

Blend the cornmeal or arrowroot and sugar to a paste with a little of the milk. Break up the chocolate or carob bar and put it into a saucepan with the rest of the milk. Heat gently for 3 to 4 minutes, or until the chocolate is melted and the milk comes to a boil. Pour a little of the boiling milk into the cornmeal or arrowroot mixture, mix well, then return to the rest of the milk in the saucepan. Return to moderate heat, stirring, until slightly thickened (2 to 3 minutes). Puree or whisk, then add the evaporated milk. Let cool, then pour into a plastic container and freeze. This ice cream sets hard, so let it stand at room temperature for 30 minutes before serving.

MILLET AND RAISIN CREAM

The old-fashioned milk puddings that our grandmothers used to make were excellent from the nutritional point of view, as well as being economical. Here is an up-to-date version based on protein- and iron-rich flaked millet, with raisins for sweetness.

Serves 4

> ½ cup flaked millet
> 2 cups milk
> ½ cup raisins
> Grated lemon rind (optional)
> 1 to 2 tablespoons honey (optional)

Put all the ingredients into a saucepan and bring to a boil. Reduce the heat to as low as possible and simmer very gently for 20 to 30 minutes, or until it has thickened. The mixture can be served hot or poured into individual serving dishes and allowed to cool. It's good with some light cream or thick plain yogurt on top.

MUESLI, ORIGINAL VERSION

Although most people think of muesli as a breakfast, it was originally a fruit dish, invented by Dr. Bircher-Benner at the turn of the century to try to get the patients at his health clinic in Zurich to eat more fresh fruit. The composition of his original dish was said to be very close to breast milk. It makes a good dish for toddlers, either as a dessert or as a main dish, and it's also good for you if you're fancying small, frequent meals when you're pregnant or breast-feeding. This is Dr. Bircher-Benner's original recipe.

Serves 1

> 1 *tablespoon sweetened condensed milk*
> 1 *tablespoon lemon juice*
> 1 *tablespoon rolled oats*
> 1 *large eating apple*
> 1 *tablespoon chopped or grated hazelnuts or almonds*
>   *(finely ground if you're giving this to a toddler)*

Put the condensed milk and lemon juice into a bowl and mix together, then add the oats. Wash the apple, then grate fairly coarsely into the bowl. If the mixture is too stiff, add a little water. Spoon into a bowl and sprinkle with the nuts. If you're serving this as a dessert, it's nice with some light cream.

IF YOU DON'T EAT DAIRY PRODUCTS. Instead of condensed milk, use soy milk or Vegan Yogurt (page 219) and add honey to taste.

MUESLI, OATY VERSION

Muesli needn't be just a cereal dish eaten at breakfast. I often make a fruity version and serve it as a pudding. This dish contains oats to help counteract depression, apples and orange juice for vitamin C, yogurt for calcium, and almonds and raisins for iron. Babies love it. Grate the apples finely and powder the oats and almonds in a blender if you're making it for a baby.

Serves 4

> 3 large apples, washed and grated (skin, core, and all)
> ½ cup orange juice
> 1 cup rolled oats
> 1 tablespoon honey
> ¼ cup raisins
> ½ cup slivered almonds, or use roasted peanuts (see page 58)
>   for economy

Put all the ingredients except the almonds or peanuts into a bowl and mix together. Spoon into bowls, then sprinkle with the nuts. This is lovely—if you want to spoil yourself—with some light cream on top.

IF YOU DON'T EAT DAIRY PRODUCTS. Use Vegan Yogurt (page 219).

PEACHES IN RASPBERRY PUREE

This is like a peach melba without the ice cream (although you could include it if you wish!). It's light, refreshing, and delicious.

Serves 4

> 2 cups fresh or frozen raspberries
> 4 ripe peaches

First make the raspberry puree: Sieve—or (preferably) puree, then sieve—the raspberries. Sweeten with honey to taste.

Put the peaches into a bowl cover with boiling water and let stand for 2 minutes. Drain and slip off the skins with a sharp knife. Halve the peaches and remove pits. Slice the peaches. Pour a pool of the raspberry sauce onto individual plates and arrange the peach slices on top.

PEAR AND CAROB TART

This is best if you can allow time for the carob crust to chill before adding the pears, but it is not essential.

Serves 6

> 2 cups cashew pieces
> ½ vanilla pod or ½ teaspoon real vanilla extract
> 2 tablespoons carob powder
> 3 tablespoons honey
> 3 to 4 ripe pears
> Juice of 1 lemon

If you've got a food processor, combine the cashew pieces, vanilla pod, carob powder, and 2 tablespoons of the honey and whizz to make a consistency that will hold together. Otherwise, grate the cashew pieces finely and add the vanilla extract, carob powder, and 2 tablespoons of the honey; mix well. Press this mixture firmly into the base and up the sides of an 8-inch removable-bottom tart dish. Chill, for an hour or so if possible, or at least while you're preparing the pears.

Peel and quarter the pears. Remove the cores, then slice the quarters into long pieces. Sprinkle the pieces with lemon juice and the remaining honey, making sure they're all coated. Arrange the pear slices in the tart. Cut in slices to serve. It's nice with some thick plain yogurt.

TOFU ICE CREAM

If you keep some strawberries in the freezer, this makes an instant dessert, but you do need a food processor.

Serves 4 to 6

> *1 pound frozen strawberries, allowed to thaw for 15 to 20*
> *   minutes*
> *½ pound firm tofu*
> *1 banana, peeled and cut into rough chunks*
> *2 tablespoons honey*

Put all the ingredients into a food processor and whizz until a thick, frozen ice cream is formed (the icy strawberries will freeze the rest of the ingredients). Serve at once, or transfer the mixture to a covered plastic container and store in the freezer. Remove the ice cream from the freezer 30 minutes or so before you want to eat it, and stir before serving.

YOGURT, BANANA, AND CRUNCHY

A quick dessert or nutritious breakfast dish or snack.

Serves 1

> *1 banana*
> *2 tablespoons plain yogurt*
> *1 to 2 tablespoons crunchy breakfast cereal*
> *Honey (optional)*

Slice the banana and put into a serving bowl. Pour the yogurt over the banana and sprinkle with the crunchy cereal. Spoon a little honey on top if you wish.

IF YOU DON'T EAT DAIRY PRODUCTS. Use Vegan Yogurt (recipe follows).

VEGAN YOGURT

Makes 2 cups

> *2 cups soy milk*
> *Yogurt starter culture*

Any yogurt culture will work as well on soy milk as it does on dairy milk. Put the soy milk into a saucepan and bring to a boil, then let cool to lukewarm. Add the starter as directed on the package, stirring well. Pour the mixture into a Thermos container or large jar or bowl that has been sterilized by being rinsed out with boiling water. Cover the jar or bowl with plastic wrap or foil and wrap in a warm towel. Leave in a warm place for 5 to 8 hours, or until set, then chill in the refrigerator. This first batch will not be 100 percent vegan, but a tablespoonful of this can be used to start the next batch, which will be. The yogurt gets thicker and better each time.

Bread, Cakes, Scones, and Biscuits

When cakes and biscuits are made with wholesome ingredients such as whole wheat flour, nuts, dried fruit, molasses, and not too much fat and sugar, they can be nutritious—rich in iron and B vitamins—as well as delicious. And strange though it may seem, they can be just what you crave, particularly in the early days of pregnancy if you're prone to sudden hunger pangs and/or nausea. These foods are also nice when you're breast-feeding, especially in the early days when your milk supply is becoming established. So don't feel guilty if you fancy something sweet; just make sure that what you have is as nourishing and wholesome as possible.

QUICK WHOLE WHEAT BREAD

You can reduce bread-making time dramatically by adding ascorbic acid or vitamin C to the dough, and this also helps reduce the phytic acid present (see pages 30–31). You can also add calcium carbonate (prepared chalk) to increase the calcium content (see page 33) and replace 2 tablespoons of the flour with the same amount of wheat germ, adding a tablespoon of molasses for an iron-rich wheat germ bread. This bread can be ready in 1 hour 45 minutes.

Makes two 1-pound loaves

>   1 ounce fresh yeast
>   1½ cups warm water
>   One 25-mg ascorbic acid tablet, crushed
>   3 cups (packed) whole wheat flour
>   1 tablespoon sea salt
>   1 teaspoon sugar
>   1 tablespoon butter or margarine, softened

Dissolve the yeast in the water and add the ascorbic acid. Mix the flour, salt, and sugar and blend in the butter or margarine. Make a well in the center, pour in the yeast liquid, and mix to form a dough. Knead for 5 to 10 minutes, then put the dough in a bowl, cover, and let stand for 5 minutes—the dough will increase by one-third. Punch the dough down, knead again briefly, then shape into loaves and place in greased loaf pans. Cover the bread and put it in a warm place until it has doubled in size, about 40 to 45 minutes. Bake in a preheated 450°F oven for 30 to 35 minutes. Test by turning the loaves out of the pans and tapping them on the base with your knuckles. If they sound hollow like a drum, they are done. If not, put them back into the oven upside down, without their pans, for 4 to 5 minutes. Let cool on a wire rack.

APRICOT, ALMOND, AND WHEAT GERM LOAF

This moist, fruity loaf is packed with fiber and contains protein, calcium, iron, and B vitamins.

Makes one 1-pound loaf

> ¼ *pound dried apricots*
> ½ *cup hot water*
> ½ *cup whole wheat flour*
> 1 *teaspoon baking powder*
> ½ *teaspoon mixed spices (such as ground cloves, nutmeg, cinnamon, and ginger)*
> ¼ *cup wheat germ*
> ½ *cup golden raisins*
> ½ *cup turbinado sugar*
> ½ *cup almonds, with skins on, chopped*
> 1 *egg, beaten*

Preheat the oven to 350°F. Wash the apricots in warm water, then shred them into small pieces with a pair of kitchen scissors or a sharp knife. Put into a bowl and cover with the hot water. Let stand while you line a 1-pound loaf pan with a strip of wax paper and grease well. Then sift the flour, baking powder, and spices together into a bowl and add the wheat germ, raisins, sugar, almonds, and egg. Now add the apricots, together with the soaking water, and mix everything together well. Spoon into the prepared loaf pan. Bake in the center of the oven for 50 to 60 minutes, or until the top springs back when touched and a skewer inserted in the middle comes out clean. Turn out onto a wire rack to cool. Serve in thick slices, with butter.

IF YOU DON'T EAT DAIRY PRODUCTS. Omit the egg, increase the baking powder to 2 teaspoons, and use 1 cup hot water. Make sure the water has cooled to tepid before you add it to the rest of the ingredients.

TO FREEZE. When completely cooled, wrap in plastic or foil and freeze. To serve, remove the wrappings and let the loaf stand on a wire rack until defrosted.

DATE SLICES

These are a good source of iron and B vitamins and are particularly satisfying. They also make a good dessert, eaten warm from the oven with some milk, cream, one of the toppings on pages 203–5, or a dollop of plain yogurt over them.

Makes 16

> ½ pound plain dates (not sugar-rolled)
> ½ cup water
> ¾ cup whole wheat flour
> 2 cups rolled oats
> 12 tablespoons (1½ sticks) margarine, softened

½ cup light brown sugar
2 tablespoons cold water

Preheat the oven to 375°F. Grease a 7¾-by-12-inch jelly roll pan. Put the dates into a saucepan with the water and heat gently for 5 to 10 minutes, or until the dates are mushy. Remove from the heat and mash with a spoon to make a thick puree, looking out for and removing any pits as you do so; set aside to let cool. Meanwhile sift the flour into a bowl, adding also the residue of bran from the sieve and the oats. Blend in the margarine with your fingertips or a fork, then add the sugar and water. Press the mixture together to form a dough. Press half the dough into the prepared tin, spread the cooled date puree on top, then cover with the remaining dough and press down gently but firmly. Bake for 30 minutes. Let cool in the tin, then cut into 16 pieces and remove with a spatula.

TO FREEZE. Pack in a covered rigid container with freezer paper between the layers; freeze. To serve, remove from container as required. They defrost very quickly and can be eaten almost immediately.

DATE AND WALNUT LOAF

This is another loaf with plenty of fiber, so it's a useful cure for constipation problems in pregnancy and after the birth. It is also a good source of B vitamins.

Makes one 1-pound loaf

1¼ cups dates
1¼ cups water
¼ cup brown sugar
¾ cup whole wheat flour
3 teaspoons baking powder
¾ cup walnuts, chopped
1 teaspoon vanilla extract

Put the dates into a saucepan with the water and simmer gently until the dates are reduced to a mush. Remove from heat and set aside to cool. Preheat the oven to 350°F. Line a 1-pound loaf pan with a strip of wax paper and grease.

Sift the flour and baking powder into a bowl, adding the residue of bran from the sieve as well. Add the sugar, walnuts, vanilla, and cooled date mixture and stir well. Spoon into the prepared loaf pan and bake for 50 to 60 minutes, or until the center feels springy and a skewer inserted into the center comes out clean. Let cool on a wire rack. Serve cut into thick slices and buttered.

TO FREEZE. When completely cooled, wrap in plastic or foil and freeze. To serve, remove the wrappings and place the loaf on a wire rack until defrosted.

WHOLE WHEAT FRUITCAKE

This fruitcake contains good quantities of iron, calcium, B vitamins, and fiber. It's a particularly good one to have in the early days of breast-feeding and will keep well in a tin for 3 to 4 weeks.

Makes one 7-inch cake

> *1¼ cups whole wheat flour*
> *2 teaspoons baking powder*
> *12 tablespoons (1½ sticks) margarine*
> *1 cup brown sugar*
> *3 eggs*
> *4 cups mixed dried fruit*
> *½ cup glacé cherries, washed and quartered (optional)*
> *Grated rind of ½ lemon*
> *Grated rind of ½ orange*
> *½ cup ground almonds*
> *¼ cup slivered almonds*

Preheat the oven to 325°F. Grease a 7-inch round cake pan and line it with greased wax paper.

Sift the flour and baking powder into a large bowl, tipping in the bran from the sieve as well. Add all the remaining ingredients except for the slivered almonds. Beat together with a wooden spoon (or with a mixer) for 2 minutes, or until light and slightly glossy looking. Spoon the mixture into the prepared cake pan, level the top, and sprinkle with the slivered almonds. Bake for 2¼ to 2½ hours, or until a skewer inserted in the center comes out clean. Let the cake cool for 15 minutes or so in the pan, then turn it out onto a wire rack, strip off the wax paper, and let stand until completely cooled. Store in an airtight tin.

TO FREEZE. Wrap the cake in plastic or foil and store in the freezer for up to 3 months. To serve, unwrap and stand the cake on a wire rack for 3 to 4 hours, or until unfrozen.

FRUITCAKE WITHOUT EGGS

An eggless fruitcake that is light and delicious. Like the preceding recipe, this cake is nutritious and good for the early breast-feeding days.

Makes one 7-inch cake

> 1 cup whole wheat flour
> 2 teaspoons baking powder
> 1 teaspoon mixed spices (ground cloves, nutmeg, cinnamon, ginger)
> 1 cup brown sugar
> 6 tablespoons oil
> 4 cups mixed dried fruit
> ½ cup glacé cherries, washed and quartered (optional)
> ¼ cup soy flour
> ¼ cup ground almonds
> 1 cup water
> ¼ cup slivered almonds

Preheat the oven to 325°F. Grease a 7-inch round cake pan and line with greased wax paper.

Sift the flour, baking powder, and spices into a large bowl, tipping in the bran from the sieve as well. Add all the remaining ingredients except for the slivered almonds. Beat together with a wooden spoon (or with a mixer) for 2 minutes, then spoon the mixture into the prepared cake pan, level the top, and sprinkle with the slivered almonds. Bake for about 2¼ hours, or until a skewer inserted in the center comes out clean. Let the cake cool for 15 minutes in the pan, then turn it out onto a wire rack, strip off the wax paper, and let stand until completely cooled. Store in an airtight tin.

TO FREEZE. Wrap the cake in plastic or foil and store in the freezer for up to 3 months. To serve, unwrap and stand the cake on a wire rack for 3 to 4 hours, or until unfrozen.

FRUIT SLICES

Easy to make, with a delicious topping of crunchy iron-rich almonds.

Makes 10 to 12

> *4 tablespoons (½ stick) margarine, softened*
> *⅔ cup brown sugar*
> *1 egg*
> *½ cup whole wheat flour*
> *2 cups mixed dried fruit*
> *¼ cup water*
> *¼ cup slivered almonds*

Preheat the oven to 325°F. Line an 8-inch square cake pan with wax paper and grease.

Put the margarine and sugar into a bowl and cream together, then beat in the egg. Add the flour, dried fruit, and water. Mix to a firm consistency; it should drop heavily from the spoon when it's tapped against the side of the bowl. If necessary, add a little more water. Spoon the mixture into the prepared cake pan, level the top, and sprinkle with the slivered almonds. Bake for about 45 minutes, or until the cake feels firm in the center. Let cool on a wire rack. Cut into 10 or 12 pieces when cooled.

PARKIN

Oatmeal is a natural remedy for depression, and both molasses and whole wheat flour contain iron. So parkin, which contains both, is useful during pregnancy and afterward as an antidote to postnatal "baby blues." If you like the flavor of molasses, you could further increase the iron content by using 2 heaping tablespoons molasses and leaving out the honey or maple syrup.

Makes 12 pieces

> *½ cup whole wheat flour*
> *2 teaspoons baking powder*
> *2 teaspoons ginger*
> *1½ cups rolled oats*
> *½ cup brown sugar*
> *¼ pound (1 stick) margarine*
> *1 big tablespoon molasses*
> *1 big tablespoon honey or maple syrup*
> *¾ cup milk*

Preheat the oven to 350°F. Line an 8-inch square cake pan with wax paper and grease.

Sift the flour, baking powder, and ginger into a bowl, tipping in the bran from the sieve as well. Add the oats. Put the sugar, margarine, molasses, and honey or maple syrup into a pan and melt over a gentle heat. Let cool until you can place your hand against the pan, then add to the flour mixture together with the milk. Mix well, then pour into the prepared cake pan. Bake for 1 hour, or until the parkin feels set in the center. Let cool in the pan, then turn out and strip off the paper. Cut into 12 pieces. Store in an airtight tin. The parkin may sink a bit in the center as it cools, but it has a wonderful moist, gooey texture and no hard "crust" on top.

IF YOU DON'T EAT DAIRY PRODUCTS. Replace the milk with soy milk.

TO FREEZE. Freeze in a rigid covered container. To serve, remove the slices as needed. Place on a wire rack until defrosted; this does not take very long.

WHOLE WHEAT SCONES WITH RAISINS AND MOLASSES

These scones have a delicious flavor and a light, crumbly texture. They're a good source of iron and are good to eat just as they are, or with butter.

Makes 8

> ½ *cup whole wheat flour*
> 2 *teaspoons baking powder*
> 2 *tablespoons margarine, softened*
> 2 *tablespoons light brown sugar*
> 1 *tablespoon rolled oats*
> ¼ *cup raisins*
> 1 *tablespoon molasses*
> ¼ *cup milk*

Preheat the oven to 350°F. Sift the flour and baking powder into a bowl, tipping in the bran from the sieve as well. Blend in the margarine with your fingertips or a fork, then add the sugar, oats, and raisins. Mix together the molasses and milk, then add this to the rest of the ingredients and mix gently to form a dough. Turn the dough out onto a lightly floured board, knead lightly, and roll out into a circle 1 inch thick. Place the circle on a floured baking sheet and score it into 8 sections. Bake for 15 minutes. Let cool in the pan, then transfer to a wire rack to finish cooling. To serve, break into individual pieces.

VARIATION
The raisins can be omitted or replaced with other dried fruit, such as golden raisins or chopped dates.

IF YOU DON'T EAT DAIRY PRODUCE. Replace milk with soy milk.

TO FREEZE. This freezes well. Wrap it unbroken in plastic or foil and freeze. To serve, remove the wrappings, stand the scone ring on a wire rack for about 1 hour to defrost. Or freeze in individual sections, which can be taken out as required and defrosted in about 15 minutes.

OATMEAL BISCUITS

This is another pleasant way of eating oats, which are a traditional herbal remedy for depression. These are plain biscuits, nice with butter and/or cheese, though I also like them just as they are.

Makes 28 to 30

> *1½ cups rolled oats*
> *½ cup whole wheat flour*
> *1 teaspoon baking powder*
> *¼ pound (1 stick) butter or margarine, softened*
> *1 tablespoon brown sugar*
> *2 tablespoons water*
> *Extra rolled oats for rolling out*

Preheat the oven to 350°F. Put the oats, flour, and baking powder into a bowl and blend in the butter or margarine. Add the sugar and water and mix to a dough. Sprinkle some oats on a board or clean working surface and roll out the dough to ¼ inch thick. Cut into 2¾-inch circles, place on a greased baking sheet, and prick lightly. Bake for 20 minutes. Let cool slightly on the baking sheet, then transfer to a wire rack. Store in an airtight tin.

TO FREEZE. When cooled, pack in a rigid covered container. Freeze for up to 3 months. To serve, remove from the container and allow to thaw on a wire rack for about 15 minutes.

Healthy Sweets
and Treats

CAROB AND CASHEW SQUARES

Makes 21

> 1 cup cashew pieces
> 1 tablespoon carob powder
> ¼ vanilla pod or a few drops real vanilla extract
> 1 tablespoon thick honey

Put the cashews, carob, and vanilla pod or extract into a blender or food processor and whizz to a powder. Then add the honey and process again to make a stiff paste. Put this into an 8-by-8-inch shallow pan and press it out so that it is ½ inch deep (it will fill only about one-third of the pan). Put into the refrigerator to harden, then cut into 21 squares.

DATE KNOBS

No extra sugar in this recipe, which is rich in fiber, iron, calcium, and B vitamins.

Makes 24

> ¼ cup dried apricots
> 1 cup plain dates (not sugar-rolled)
> ¼ cup water
> ½ cup raisins
> ½ cup mixed nuts (almonds, Brazil nuts, roasted peanuts)

Wash the apricots well in warm water, then chop. Put into a saucepan with the dates and water. Heat gently for 15 minutes, or until soft; remove any pits. Place in a blender or food processor along with the raisins and nuts and whizz to a puree. Press the mixture into a lightly greased cake pan, making it about ½ inch deep. Chill, then cut into 24 squares.

TO FREEZE. Place in rigid covered container and freeze. Take out individually as required; they can be eaten within a few minutes.

FRUITY SQUARES

Makes 64

> *1½ cups mixed dried fruit (dates, peaches, apricots, raisins)*
> *1 cup nuts (cashews, almonds, walnuts, or Brazil nuts)*
> *1 cup dried coconut (unsweetened)*
> *Grated rind of 1 orange or lemon*
> *A little orange juice*
> *Extra dried coconut*

Put the dried fruit and nuts into a food processor and process until finely chopped. Add the coconut and grated rind and process again, adding enough orange juice to make a firm paste. Sprinkle a little coconut in an 8-inch square cake pan, press the fruit mixture on top, then sprinkle with more coconut and press down well. Put a weight on top and place in the refrigerator to harden. Cut into 1-inch squares.

NUTTY CAROB BANANAS

These are a healthy and absolutely delicious version of ice pops.

Makes 3

> *1 large banana*
> *3 Popsicle sticks*
> *Honey*
> *Chopped nuts*
> *Carob powder*

Peel the banana and cut into 3 crosswise pieces. Insert a Popsicle stick into each. Spread the honey, nuts, and carob powder on 3 separate flat dishes. Dip the banana pieces first into the honey to coat completely, then into the nuts, then into the carob powder. Place on a platter or baking sheet in freezer and freeze until firm for about 1 hour.

. . . .

Appendix

TABLE A
SUMMARY OF NUTRIENTS: WHERE THEY ARE AND
WHAT THEY DO

NUTRIENT	MAIN SOURCES	FUNCTION
Protein	Milk; cheese; yogurt, eggs; legumes, including soy flour, tofu, and soy milk; nuts and seeds; cereals, whole-grain bread; wheat germ	Growth and repair of body cells. Reproduction and formation of blood and bones. Protection against infection.
Fiber	Legumes, nuts and seeds, whole-grain cereals, fresh and dried fruits, vegetables	Healthy functioning of the digestive system.
Fat	Oil, butter, margarine, whole milk, cream, yogurt, vegetable fats, egg yolk, cheese, nuts and seeds, avocado	Production of hormones and bile acids. Health of membranes. Polyunsaturated fats help absorption of vitamins A, D, and E. Source of energy.
Fat-Soluble Vitamins Vitamin A	Egg yolk, dairy products, fortified margarine, carrots, apricots, oranges, tomatoes, yellow and orange melons, peaches, mangos, tomatoes, all green and some yellow vegetables	Healthy eyes, skin, lungs, throat, hair, and nails. Increases resistance to infection. Helps in the healing process.

TABLE A
SUMMARY OF NUTRIENTS: WHERE THEY ARE AND WHAT THEY DO

NUTRIENT	MAIN SOURCES	FUNCTION
Vitamin D	Butter, margarine, cottage cheese, yogurt, milk, evaporated milk, hard cheese, egg, action of sunlight on skin	Absorption of calcium for bones and teeth.
Vitamin E	Whole-grain cereals, wheat germ, nuts, seeds, green leafy vegetables, legumes; cold-pressed vegetable oils (richest sources)	Improves general vitality and is important for proper functioning of the heart and cell structures
Vitamin K	Green leafy vegetables, soy bean oil, tomatoes, egg yolk, alfalfa	Blood clotting and prevention of excess loss of blood after injuries.
Water-Soluble Vitamins B Complex B1 Thiamin	Whole-grain bread, wheat germ, fortified breakfast cereals, brewers' yeast, yeast extract, peanuts, Brazil nuts, legumes, soy flour, oranges, dried egg yolk, dairy products	Involved in the release of energy from starch and sugars, and for the health of muscles, nerves, eyes, hair, skin, and blood.
B_2 (Riboflavin)	Fortified breakfast cereals, brewers' yeast, yeast extract,	Proper metabolism of starches and sugars, production

TABLE A
SUMMARY OF NUTRIENTS: WHERE THEY ARE AND
WHAT THEY DO

NUTRIENT	MAIN SOURCES	FUNCTION
	almonds, wheat germ, dairy products, dark green leafy vegetables, mushrooms, potatoes, dried fruit, avocado, chocolate	of antibodies, and healthy function and development of the brain.
Niacin	Fortified breakfast cereals, wheat germ, whole-grain bread, milk and milk products, brewers' yeast, yeast extract, peanuts, almonds, leafy vegetables, mushrooms, avocado, chocolate, dried fruit (especially figs, apricots, prunes and peaches), legumes	Similar to riboflavin.
B_6 (pyridoxine)	Brewers' yeast, yeast extract, whole-grain bread, wheat germ, soy flour, walnuts, peanuts, legumes, eggs, milk, corn, sprouts, bananas	Utilization of protein and production of hemoglobin.

TABLE A
SUMMARY OF NUTRIENTS: WHERE THEY ARE AND
WHAT THEY DO

NUTRIENT	MAIN SOURCES	FUNCTION
Vitamin B_{12}	Dairy products, fortified foods, yeast extract	Similar to vitamins B_1, B_2, and niacin. Also for production of bone marrow.
Folic Acid	Wheat germ, brewers' yeast, yeast extract, dark green leafy vegetables, raw peanuts and walnuts, raw cauliflower, mushrooms, tomatoes, oranges, potatoes, most fruit and vegetables, cow's milk (not goat's), eggs	Works with vitamin B_{12} in cell division. Vital in pregnancy.
Pantothenic Acid	Brewers' yeast, yeast extract, eggs, peanuts, wheat germ, mushrooms, whole-grain bread and cereals, cheese, legumes	Release of energy from food. Proper functioning of adrenal glands.
Vitamin C (Ascorbic Acid)	Oranges, grapefruit, strawberries, tomatoes, green leafy vegetables, potatoes, bean sprouts, red peppers	Increases resistance to infection. Helps in the healing process. Promotes normal growth.

TABLE A
SUMMARY OF NUTRIENTS: WHERE THEY ARE AND
WHAT THEY DO

NUTRIENT	MAIN SOURCES	FUNCTION
Minerals Calcium	Milk, cheese, yogurt, legumes, sesame seeds, blackstrap molasses, sunflower seeds, almonds, green leafy vegetables (especially broccoli and spinach); carob, soy flour and milk, tofu, dried fruit (especially figs), brewers' yeast	Maintenance of healthy bones and teeth. Blood clotting. Healthy working of heart and skin.
Iron	Brewers' yeast, blackstrap molasses, legumes, soy flour and milk, tofu, green leafy vegetables, dried fruits, whole-grain bread and whole grains, almonds, pumpkin seeds, eggs	Healthy blood. (Absorption aided by foods containing vitamin C.)

TABLE A
SUMMARY OF NUTRIENTS: WHERE THEY ARE AND
WHAT THEY DO

NUTRIENT	MAIN SOURCES	FUNCTION
Magnesium	Whole grains, whole-grain bread, wheat germ, nuts (especially almonds, cashews, Brazil nuts), legumes, soy flour, tofu, soy milk, brewers' yeast, fruit (especially bananas), vegetables (especially potatoes and leafy greens)	Release of energy from carbohydrates. Healthy formation of bones and teeth.
Phosphorus	Usually present with calcium	Used with calcium for healthy bones and teeth.
Potassium	In nearly all foods, especially vegetables, legumes, fruits, whole-grain bread, brewers' yeast, nuts, and seeds	Healthy cells, growth, and health of the heart.
Sodium	Table salt, sea salt, miso, tamari and shoyu soy sauce, celery, cheeses, nuts, egg yolk, dairy products	Many vital body functions.
Trace Elements Zinc	Nuts, pumpkin seeds, dairy produce, eggs, brewers' yeast,	Normal growth and healing.

TABLE A
SUMMARY OF NUTRIENTS: WHERE THEY ARE AND WHAT THEY DO

NUTRIENT	MAIN SOURCES	FUNCTION
	legumes, peas, asparagus, spinach, cauliflower, mushrooms, mangos, whole-grain bread, whole-grain cereals	
Iodine	Seaweeds, including vegetarian jelling agents; soybeans, iodized salt, garlic, green vegetables	Needed by the thyroid gland.
Manganese	Whole-grain bread, wheat germ, whole-grain cereals, nuts, dried figs, dates, peaches, apricots, brewers' yeast	Utilization of vitamin B_1. Also needed in reproduction and lactation.

TABLE B
HOW IT ALL ADDS UP: ANALYSIS OF ONE DAY'S VEGETARIAN MENUS
This analysis is based on the day's meal plan given on pages 43–46. I've calculated the
nutritional values for the staple foods to demonstrate how these can meet the daily
requirements. I have purposely chosen simple, inexpensive basic foods. You would almost
certainly enliven meals with some butter, margarine, or oil as well as extra fruits and
vegetables, such as a little carrot or tomato, perhaps an apple or banana, thus increasing the
calorie value and adding further nutrients.

FOOD	WEIGHT	CALO-RIES	FIBER (IN G)	PRO-TEIN (IN G)	VIT. A (IN IU)	B_1 (IN MG)	B_2 (IN MG)
4 slices whole-grain bread	3 ounces	342	1.6	4.8	tr	0.24	0.08
2 tablespoons butter[a]	1 ounce	204	0	0.1	940	tr	0.02
1 cup rolled oats, raw	1½ ounces	161	3.0	2.5	tr[b]	0.2	0.04
¼ cup wheat germ	9/10 ounce	74	—	6.6	0	0.5	0.2
¼ cup almonds	1⅓ ounces	167	1.0	7.3	0	0.09	0
¼ cup pumpkin seeds	1⅓ ounces	155	0.5	10.1	20	0.07	0.05
2 dried figs	1¾ ounces	107	9.2	2.2	32	0.05	0.03
½ cup cooked lima beans	3½ ounces	131	7.0	7.8	160	0.13	0.06
1 cup cooked brown rice	6 ounces	178	3.6	8.0	0	0.14	0.30
3 tablespoons peanut butter	1½ ounces	258	1.0	11.7	0	0.05	0.06
1½ cups low-fat milk[d]	14 ounces	181	0	12.9	225	0.14	0.6
1 cup sprouts, cooked	5 ounces	56	6.5	3.72	810	0.12	0.22
1 orange	6 ounces	64	0.9	1.3	260	0.13	0.05
1 large carrot, raw	3½ ounces	42	3.0	1.1	11,000	0.06	0.05
1 tablespoon brewers' yeast	⅓ ounce	23	0.14	3.1	tr	1.25	0.34
Total	—	2,143	37.44	88.12	13,447	2.17	2.05
RDA for Average Woman		2,200	35	44	4,000	1.0	1.2

[a]Or vegetable margarine, which adds 2.5 mg of vitamin E.
[b]Unless fortified with this vitamin.
[c]Estimate.
[d]Vegans would use fortified soy milk instead of dairy milk. This would increase the riboflavin
a little and add around 2 mg iron and 5.5 mcg B_{12} (check your own brand), but only give 72
mg calcium. This could be increased by serving extra soy milk, broccoli instead of (or as well
as) sprouts, or a little tofu or tahini or a couple of extra figs, or in any of the ways described
on page 33. The extra fruits and vegetables which would probably be added to the basic foods
could also add some calcium.
NOTE: A dash means the information is not available.

TABLE B (continued)

B$_6$ (IN MG)	B$_{12}$ (IN MCG)	FOLIC ACID (IN MCG)	NIACIN (IN MG)	VIT. C (IN MG)	VIT. E (IN MG)	CA (IN MG)	FE (IN MG)	MG (IN MG)	ZN (IN MG)
0.16	0	85	2.4	0	2.0	92	2.00	72	2.0
—	tr	—	—	—	0.7	6	0	tr	0.2
0.04	0	140	0.4	0	0.1	23	1.7	38	0.6
0.23	0	66	1.05	0	3.0	18	2.3	84	3.6
0.01	0	13	1.25	tr	4.2	83	1.7	96	1.0
—	0	29	0.68	—	—	18	3.9	—	—
0.16	0	15	0.8	0	—	63	1.5	35	—
0.15	0	160^c	0.65	—	—	28	3.0	32	0.85
0.3^c	0	—	9.2	0	0.5^c	18	0.8	90	0.8
0.15	0	26	7.2	0	2.93	33	0.9	78	1.5^c
0.15	4.5	18	0.32	3	0	453	0.18	50	1.43
0.28	0	56	1.2	135	1.0	50	1.7	2	0.54
0.11	0	83	0.5	66	0.43	54	0.5	20	0.26
0.15	—	—	0.6	8	0.45	37	0.7	23	0.4
0.2	0^b	192	3.0	tr	0	17	1.4	19	0.44
1.09	4.5	793	29.2	212	15.31	1,003	21.78	639	13.62
2.0	3.0	400	13	60	8	800	18	300	15

TABLE C
RECOMMENDED DAILY DIETARY ALLOWANCES FOR WOMEN
(REVISED 1980)
(Adapted from the Food and Nutrition Board of the National Academy of Sciences/National Research Council)

				FAT-SOLUBLE VITAMINS			WATER-SOLUBLE VITAMINS		
AGE	WEIGHT	HEIGHT	PRO-TEIN	VITA-MIN A	VITA-MIN D	VITA-MIN E	VITA-MIN C	THIA-MINE	RIBO-FLAVIN
(years)	(pounds)	(inches)	(g)	(IU)	(mcg)	(mg)	(mg)	(mg)	(mg)
11–14	101	62	46	4,000	10	8	50	1.1	1.3
15–18	120	64	46	4,000	10	8	60	1.1	1.3
19–22	120	64	44	4,000	7.5	8	60	1.1	1.3
23–50	120	64	44	4,000	5	8	60	1.0	1.2
Pregnant			+30	5,000	+5	+2	+20	+0.4	+0.3
Lactating			+20	6,000	+5	+3	+40	+0.5	+0.5

*The increased requirement during pregnancy cannot be met by the iron content of typical American diets nor by the existing iron stores of many women. Therefore, the use of 30 to 60 mg of supplemental iron is recommended. Iron needs during lactation are not substantially different from those of nonpregnant women, but continued supplementation for mothers for two to three months after parturition is advisable to replenish stores depleted by pregnancy.

TABLE C (continued)

					MINERALS				
NIA-CIN	VITA-MIN B$_6$	FOLIC ACID	VITA-MIN B$_{12}$	CALCIUM	PHOS-PHORUS	MAGNE-SIUM	IRON	ZINC	IO-DINE
(mg)	(mg)	(mcg)	(mcg)	(mg)	(mg)	(mg)	(mg)	(mg)	(mcg)
15	1.8	400	3.0	1200	1200	300	18	15	150
14	2.0	400	3.0	1200	1200	300	18	15	150
14	2.0	400	3.0	800	800	300	18	15	150
13	2.0	400	3.0	800	800	300	18	15	150
+2	+0.6	+400	+1.0	+400	+400	+150	*	+5	+25
+5	+0.5	+100	+1.0	+400	+400	+150	*	+10	+50

Index

About the Author

Rose Elliot, a vegetarian since the age of three, is one of England's most popular cookbook authors. Her many best-selling books include *The Festive Vegetarian, Vegetarian Dishes from Around the World,* and *The Complete Vegetarian Cuisine.* An active food consultant, she has appeared often on television and radio in Britain. She lives in Hampshire, England.